Quantum Publishing Group, A division of Appit Ventures,
LLC
Denver, Colorado
www.QuantumPublishingGroup.com

Cover design by Nicole Demetrick

Disclaimer: Neither the author or the publisher is in any way
advising for any kind of psychological treatment. This book is
not intended to substitute for psychiatric or medical care.

ISBN: 978-0-9898341-2-4

Life, Reinvented

A Guide to Healing from Sexual Trauma for
Survivors and Loved Ones

By

Erin Carpenter, LCSW

Acknowledgments

I would like to thank my amazing husband and family for their unfailing support. I am also grateful for every teacher, professor, and mentor whom I have had the pleasure of working with, especially Christopher Duessing and Maria Antonaccio.

To the brave and insightful survivors that allowed me to be a part of their healing process, this book would not have been possible without you. I am humbled by your courage and grit. Health, wholeness, and happiness are your birthright. Keep striving.

Table of Contents

Rape and Sexual Assault Myths
The Impact of Myth
What if I Didn't Fight Back, Yell Out, or Ask For
Help?
What if I Went Along With It Because I Was Afraid or
Shocked?
What if I Didn't Stop It Because I Was Just Used To
It?
What if I Enjoyed It?
Survivors Speak—Madison

Common Trauma-related Effects
Re-experiencing the Trauma
Rumination
Hyperarousal
Avoidance and Numbing
Dissociation
Relationship Problems
A Note to Loved Ones
Identity Problems
Spiritual Problems
Survivors Speak—Vivian

Post-Traumatic Stress Disorder (PTSD)
Complex Post-Traumatic Stress Disorder
Dissociative Disorders
Generalized Anxiety Disorder (GAD)

The Listener-Not the Fixer
The Mirror
The Encourager
The Boundary-Setter
Dos and Don'ts
What about Me?
When to Get Help
For Intimate Partners
Loved Ones Speak—Mark

Introduction

This book is written for survivors of sexual trauma and their loved ones. If you are a survivor, I know it is a big step to simply pick up this book. The very first task in healing is lifting the veil of denial and accepting what has happened in your life. By reading this book, you have already begun to heal.

The fact that you picked up this book means that some part of you is in pain. Even if you do not yet completely understand your trauma, something in you resonated with this title. I hope that you honor that. Whatever pain is crying out for your attention, I hope that you are able to listen.

This book is meant to be informative, relatively free of psychological jargon, and accessible to anyone. I wrote this book with my clients in mind. They challenge and inspire me, and I am grateful to be a part of their healing. Inside this book is everything I would wish a survivor to know.

But simply conveying information is not my greatest ambition for this book. My greatest goal is that as you read these words you feel validated in your experience, and, ultimately, that you feel hope. Hope is a valuable commodity to those who have been traumatized and betrayed. If I could convey one thing to you, it would be this: you can feel differently than you do right now. People are incredibly resilient, and I see courageous survivors heal a bit more each day. Everyone naturally strives towards health and wholeness, even in the midst of pain and suffering.

I spoke about my greatest hope for this book, but I also want to mention my greatest fear. My greatest fear is that you may not find all of your experience reflected in these pages. I wanted to write a concise and accessible book, and could not possibly include all of the different ways people experience sexual trauma. Everyone is an individual. If you do not see yourself in these pages, that does not mean your experience is invalid or abnormal. People have varied responses to trauma.

If you are a loved one of a survivor, I hope this book helps you understand how they may be feeling and what you can do to help. I want to thank you on behalf of the survivor in your life. Sexual trauma is misunderstood, and you are taking time and energy to educate yourself. Many of my clients wish their friends, romantic partners, co-workers, and family knew more about the issue. They grow weary of teaching them how to be helpful. Your support, understanding, and patience are invaluable. The last chapter is focused on you. In it, your experience is validated and I offer helpful tools and tips for supporting your survivor.

In this book I've included many first-hand survivor stories. All names and identifying details have been changed to protect confidentiality. I hope that these stories give you validation, hope, and comfort.

I feel honored to have been a small part of many people's healing. I hope this book can be a part of your healing as well.

Chapter 1: What Just Happened? The Difficulty of Definition

Sexual trauma, which I use as a term to encompass sexual abuse, sexual assault, molestation, and rape, is more common than is conscionable. It is estimated that 1 in 6 women will be the victim of a completed or attempted rape in her lifetime. For men, the number is 1 in 33.[i] Of all victims, almost half are under the age of 18 and 15% are under the age of 12.[ii]

No matter what happened, when it happened, or with whom, there is one thing that remains the same: it's hard to believe. Sexual trauma is an event that shatters your world, sense of safety, and implicit trust in others. Your boundaries are violated in the most intrusive way imaginable. It robs you of a sense of control over your body and calls into question your entire sense of who you are.

We are natural meaning-makers. Everything that happens in our lives is usually integrated into one long narrative about ourselves, others, and the world we inhabit. If we didn't have the capacity to make sense of our lives, we would be forever in confusion. Sexual trauma throws a big wrench in this system. We try in vain to make sense of what happened, and of the feelings and thoughts that are left in its wake.

It is very difficult to weave an incident like sexual assault into the rest of our experience, and, as a result, we have a hard time seeing it for what it really is. We forget it, repress it, or minimize it. We justify it or blame ourselves or outright deny it. And every time we think it has found a place to rest, it springs up again. It comes screaming at us and we can't look away.

This chapter is about what happened. It's about saying the word aloud, even if it's only to yourself. We will explore the myths about sexual trauma and challenge that little voice inside you that whispers, "It's my fault...I let it happen...I shouldn't have been drinking...I should have known it was wrong..."

The first step toward recovery is the choice to face reality. In many ways, the symptoms that survivors experience are the body and mind's way of forcing you to look at what happened. Memories of sexual trauma seem to rocket around the brains of survivors, refusing to be at rest and constantly putting themselves at the forefront of the survivors' minds. The body also holds trauma that expresses itself in many ways. The body and mind work together to force survivors to relate directly to their past experiences. That is, to have a relationship to the past that is free of denial, repression, or distortion. This is a painful process, but it is the only way forward.

—

Sexual Trauma Myths

The incidence of sexual trauma in our society is disturbing. By any measure, it is relatively common and threatens to affect each individual's family, friends, neighbors, and co-workers. Because we are so uncomfortable with this idea, we create a mythology around sexual trauma. We tell ourselves stories about who victims are, what they do or don't do, where and when these assaults occur, and what perpetrators are like. This keeps us comfortable and distanced from the reality of these experiences.

Unfortunately, the survivors of sexual trauma pay the costs of these myths. Survivors believe in them, just like everyone else. These myths and ill-informed attitudes serve to keep survivors in a place of shame, guilt, and isolation. Many of the men and women I have seen over the years feel intensely isolated, alone, and misunderstood because of their trauma.

As I often tell my clients, the "comparison monster" is nearly always with us. We are constantly comparing our experiences with others', or what we believe their experiences to be. This allows us to gauge if we are "normal" or not. Everyone in our society understands a basic template about sexual violence. Unfortunately, the widely understood

—

definition of sexual violence is at odds with the real world. Survivors are often comparing their experience of sexual assault, rape, or molestation with their ideas garnered from movies, TV, books, news reports, etc. When someone's experience doesn't "match up" (and it most often does not), they are left feeling confused. They often believe their trauma-related difficulties are somehow invalid. It's as if what happened to them wasn't "real rape" or "legitimate abuse."

As people work through their trauma and heal, they tend to compare less and less. Survivors begin to accept their experience for what it is, and learn to validate their own thoughts and feelings. I usually begin work with survivors by exploring their beliefs about sexual violence and exposing the myths that serve to make survivors feel alienated and alone.

You have probably heard all of the following myths about sexual trauma. As you read through them, take a moment to check in with yourself. Do you believe these myths? Does your actual experience match them? How have these myths served to increase your own self-blame and confusion?

Myth 1: Only women are raped or sexually abused, and only men are abusers.

In my therapy practice, I have had the privilege of

working with many courageous men who are survivors of sexual abuse which they suffered as children, sexual assault as an adult, or both. They often feel very alone and ashamed about what happened to them. Approximately one in six boys will be sexually abused in some way before the age of sixteen. iii

Abusers are not always men. Women have been found to abuse both males and females. The idea that a man cannot be molested or raped by a woman is a myth. Any time there is non-consensual sexual activity there is rape. Often men struggle with the praise they receive, both implicitly and explicitly, for having sex. Men may be confused about a sexual experience they didn't want and then received praise for. I have worked with many men who expressed both confusion and pain because their actual experience clashes with society's expectation of them.

Women can also be abused by other women, and this happens often. These women often feel guilt, shame, and confusion because their experience does not match the stereotypical male-on-female sexual assault. This experience is real sexual violence, and is made all the more painful because the survivor feels alone and misunderstood.

Myth 2: Being assaulted or raped by someone of the same gender means the survivor is, or could become, gay.

—

This is not true. Sexual violence is ultimately not about pleasure; it is about power. Perpetrators like to be in control and to have power over others. Perpetrators are interested in getting what they want, not in their victim's sexual orientation. I have seen, in my practice, many courageous survivors of different sexual orientations. Your sexual orientation is about what feels pleasurable and safe for you, and about your identity. Ultimately, it has no relationship with the gender of your abuser.

Myth 3: Someone who is drinking or using drugs is at least partly to blame for a sexual assault.

The victim of sexual violence is never to blame, no matter what their behavior. Under almost all state laws, someone who is significantly intoxicated cannot consent to sexual contact.[iv] In all states, an unconscious person cannot give consent. Consent, legally defined, reflects an act of free will and knowledge of the nature of the act. It is the perpetrator who is to blame for not obtaining consent, for taking advantage of someone who is vulnerable, or for using substances to facilitate their own desires. When someone chooses to drink or use drugs, they choose to use substances; they do not choose to have sex.

Myth 4: It's not rape if a couple is dating or married.

Sexual assault and rape is defined by unwanted sexual contact. It does not matter if the perpetrator is a boyfriend, girlfriend, spouse, or ex-partner. Under most state laws, a prior relationship does not imply consent for sexual activity. Consent must be given for each sexual encounter. Rape can and does happen within a relationship.

Myth 5: Most survivors are raped by a stranger in a dangerous area.

This could not be further from the truth. The overwhelming majority of survivors were assaulted by someone they know: a friend, acquaintance, relative, or someone they dated.

This fact can lead to survivors feeling guilty that they should have "known better" or somehow seen "red flags" in their perpetrator's behavior before the assault. In reality I think the opposite is true. Our guard is down when we're around people we know and trust. Friends, family members, colleagues, boyfriends, or girlfriends who commit sexual assault have violated the victim's trust. This sense of betrayal can lead survivors of sexual violence to have difficulty trusting others.

Myth 6: If someone is dressing or acting in a sexual manner, they are "asking for it" and deserve some of the blame.

This is absolutely not true. No woman or man asks to be sexually assaulted. This harmful myth shifts the blame of the assault from the perpetrator to the victim. Anyone should be able to choose what he or she wears without fear of being raped or molested. Blaming articles of clothing or body language for such a violent, devastating act is absurd and, in my view, childish.

Usually this myth is applied to women. Our culture may say that a woman acting or dressing in a provocative way was signaling she wanted to have sex, and therefore was not raped. This attitude assumes that sexual violence is about sexual pleasure (it's not), and that men simply are not in control of their behavior when they are aroused. This is, of course, not at all true. Men have said about this myth (and I agree) that it is very debasing and insulting to them to assume they have no control over their behavior.

I have facilitated many workshops for the loved ones of survivors. This includes family members, romantic partners, and friends who are interested in learning more about how they can support survivors. In order to illustrate how the survivor of sexual violence experiences this kind of victim blaming, I present the case of Mr. Smith.[v] This is a short dialogue that is a teaching tool and has been around for a long time. I find it a powerful and approachable way to understand the prejudice that most survivors feel.

In the following situation, a holdup victim is asked questions by a lawyer.

Laywer: "Mr. Smith, you were held up at gunpoint on the corner of First and Main?"

Mr. Smith: "Yes."

Laywer: "Did you struggle with the robber?"

Mr. Smith: "No."

Laywer: "Why not?"

Mr. Smith: "He was armed."

Laywer: "Then you made a conscious decision to comply with his demands rather than resist?"

Mr. Smith: "Yes."

Laywer: "Did you scream? Cry out?"

Mr. Smith: "No, I was afraid."

Laywer: "I see. Have you ever been held up before?"

Mr. Smith: "No."

Laywer: "Have you ever given money away?"

Mr. Smith: "Yes, of course."

Laywer: "And you did so willingly?"

Mr. Smith: "What are you getting at?"

Laywer: "Well, let's put it like this, Mr. Smith. You've given money away in the past. In fact, you have quite a reputation for philanthropy. How can we be sure that you weren't contriving to have your money taken from you by force?"

Mr. Smith: "Listen, if I wanted—"

Laywer: "Never mind. What time did this holdup take place, Mr. Smith?"

Mr. Smith: "About 11:00 P.M."

Laywer: "You were out on the street at 11:00 P.M.? Doing what?"

Mr. Smith: "Just walking."

Laywer: "Just walking? You know that it's dangerous being out on the street that late at night. Weren't you aware that you could have been held up?"

Mr. Smith: "I hadn't thought about it."

Laywer: "What were you wearing at the time, Mr. Smith?"

Mr. Smith: "Let's see…a suit. Yes, a suit."

Laywer: "An expensive suit?"

Mr. Smith: "Well—yes. I'm a successful lawyer."

Laywer: "In other words, Mr. Smith, you were walking around the streets late at night in a suit that practically advertised the fact that you might be a good target for some easy money, isn't that so? I mean, if we didn't know better, Mr. Smith, we might even think you were asking for this to happen, mightn't we?"

Just like Mr. Smith was at least partly blamed for being robbed, survivors of sexual assault are sometimes blamed for their own trauma. Often the people around them focus on their behavior rather than the perpetrators'. This is wholly unfair and not reflective of the reality of sexual assault. Rape happens because a perpetrator makes a choice to violate their victim, and the victim's choices are in no way to blame.

Myth 7: Rape is only defined by vaginal or anal penetration.

Rape and sexual assault are defined by any unwanted sexual contact. This can include groping, oral sex, exposing oneself in a sexual way, kissing, rubbing oneself on another, or any other type of sexual touch.

Sexual molestation and sexual abuse of a child can include exposing the child to sexual material, speaking about the child in a sexual way, manipulating a child to satisfy an adult's sexual needs, or any other behavior that treats a child like a sexual object.

The Impact of Myth

The fact is that most people's experience of sexual

violence bears little resemblance to what the media portrays as rape and sexual assault. Usually, the collective imagination of rape is very narrow. The reality of sexual assault is in fact quite broad. Many different experiences qualify for this tragic label.

Sometimes when a client struggles to grasp the reality of what has happened to them, I direct them away from their intellect and toward their feelings. When sexual violence occurs, you *feel* as if something very wrong has just happened. Your boundaries are violated. You feel dirty, used, confused, and unsteady. You feel intense blame and shame. You feel alone and isolated. It feels like you can't tell anyone. These are all clues that something truly destructive has happened.

The beginning of healing usually starts here, by letting go of the myths and misconceptions. We begin by accepting a very sad truth. It's not easy. Even if we have disposed of the myths, there are still troublesome questions.

What if I didn't fight back, yell out, or ask for help?

In a later chapter, trauma's impact on the brain will be explored further (see Chapter 4). For now, we need to realize that our ability to fight off an attacker or call for help is compromised during a traumatic event. During a sexual assault our body and brain react as if we are under threat (because we are). Most often, instead of the "fight-or-flight" response that many people know about, our body goes into "freeze" mode. We freeze when our body and brain sense that fighting or running away are not realistic options for us. This is a decision that happens below our conscious awareness, meaning that it is not a choice.

When we freeze, we cannot respond. We just freeze, and our brain literally paralyzes our body so that we cannot move. This is called *tonic immobility*, and it is very common during a sexual assault.[vi] We see this in nature when an animal will "play dead."

If you did not fight back, yell out, or even utter a sound during your assault it was because you literally could not do so. The absence of a "no" is not a "yes." The absence of a struggle does not imply consent.

What if I went along with it because I was afraid or shocked?

When we are under threat, our survival mode kicks in. Just like the freeze response will emerge as a survival tactic, sometimes we sense that pretending we are compliant will make our attacker less violent or will simply get the horrific act over with. A perpetrator is more dangerous when they are afraid, angry, or unpredictable. In some cases, resisting an attacker may antagonize them. It doesn't matter what the victim's actions were during the assault; they did what they had to do to survive, both mentally and physically. It's important to realize that not physically resisting an assault does not equate to participation.

What if I didn't stop it because I was just used to it?

I mostly hear this question from survivors of childhood sexual abuse, but also from survivors of multiple assaults. When there are multiple attacks and breaches of boundaries, the victim, sadly, becomes accustomed to the abuse. He or she realizes (consciously or subconsciously) that they have no control over this situation and become passive or hopeless. Becoming accustomed to abuse is another survival mechanism. In a way, our body and brain shut down so that we can continue to live through abuse we cannot stop or control.

Appearing to tolerate abuse does not imply consent, participation, or approval. For clients that struggle with this very valid question, I try to convey that they had the immense wisdom (usually at an early age) to shut down some part of themselves and simply get through that period in their lives. During the healing process, the survivor may find a way to re-connect with and reclaim this vulnerable part of him or herself.

What if I enjoyed it?

I see two issues involved in this question, which may or may not occur together: first, an emotional bond with the perpetrator, and secondly, the way a victim's body responds to sexual violence.

To address the first issue, we need to realize that intense emotional attachment can occur within a trauma-based relationship. This kind of attachment most often occurs between the victim of childhood sexual assault and their abuser, especially if the abuser is a parent or other trusted adult. The term *trauma-bonding* was coined to describe a relationship that alternated between abuse and caretaking[vii]. This push-and-pull type of relationship creates dependency and fear in the victim that results in very ambivalent feelings about the abuser. If you hate your abuser for what they did to you, but also find yourself having positive feelings towards them, that is very normal if viewed within the lens of trauma. Enjoying parts of the abuse itself is also normal. It's often the case that the only time a child may have gotten any attention or affection was within the frame of abuse. Starved for connection and praise, a child may seek out the abuser, even while a part of them feels it is wrong. Trauma-bonding can also occur between romantic partners and is often paired with domestic violence.

The second issue is one that causes survivors a tremendous amount of guilt and shame. It is very normal during a sexual assault for one's body to react in a pleasurable way. This is very confusing and embarrassing. I am often asked in a hushed voice by my clients if part of them was sexually attracted to the perpetrator or desired the abuse because their bodies responded during the assault. My answer is always and unequivocally *no*. Our bodies are wired to react in a certain way when stimulated, and it does not imply consent or desire. I often tell my clients that the only thing their bodily response implies is that they have a healthy, functioning nervous system.

Survivors Speak-Madison, Age 22

When I first arrived at my therapist's office, I wasn't even sure that I should be there. I remember looking at the floor a lot. I was waging a fierce internal battle. Even after I had picked up the phone to call a therapist that specializes in sexual trauma, the war raged on.

I was raped when I was 20 years old. I was in college, and was out partying with my friends. I was drinking, and I was a little tipsy. One of my guy friends was there too. I didn't know him really well, but he was in our group.

20

He started to flirt with me, and I was enjoying the attention. I went back to my apartment with my roommates and some of our friends. He came along too. I don't remember exactly what happened, but he was in my bed. He began to force himself on me, and I remember just freezing. I was so shocked and I was so scared in that moment. For almost a year afterwards I blamed myself for not doing anything to stop him. I imagined how I could have kicked him, or yelled for my roommates. I didn't do any of those things. I couldn't move a muscle.

I remember waking up naked, and he was there. I felt so ashamed and disgusted. I dressed and left my house and didn't come back until that night. I was so embarrassed and I didn't want to see this guy. My roommates never asked about it.

I didn't really know what to think about what happened. Honestly, the word 'rape' never entered my mind until months later. I kept having flashbacks and nightmares about that night and feeling him on top of me. I felt traumatized, and I knew that this was a new feeling. I've had sexual experiences that weren't very pleasurable. I've regretted having sex with certain people. But this was wholly different. I knew that something wasn't right about that night, but I couldn't put my finger on it.

When I first entertained the thought of sexually assault, I dismissed it. What happened to me didn't resemble my idea of rape. There was no dark alley, no creepy stranger. And I felt I was to blame because I had been drinking that night. I wondered if I had put myself in a situation that was dangerous. I worried that if I told anyone, they would say it wasn't "real rape." I was terrified that they would say what I believed deep down—that I was asking for it.

For me, things had to get pretty bad before I reached out for help. I couldn't stop thinking about that night. I stopped going to class and stopped taking care of myself. I felt extremely depressed and isolated myself.

When I finally found myself in a therapist's office, I had a lot of misconceptions to work through. I learned a lot about sexual assault. Even when I intellectually understood that the assault was not my fault, the guilt lingered. That little voice that said it was my fault and peppered me with "what ifs" stayed around for a while. Getting myself to say the word 'rape' and to let go of my preconceived notions was the first step in healing.

It's been two years since that night. While I wouldn't consider myself healed completely, I have come a long way. The rape is something that happened to me; it doesn't define me. It's found a resting place now. The rape will always be a part of my life, but now I think much more about my future than my past.

The Difficulty of Definition

Chapter 2: Am I Going Crazy? Symptoms as a Normal Response to an Abnormal Situation

Any survivor of a traumatic event carries the effects of that trauma with them. In psychological terms, these effects are called *symptoms*, but I think that's a misleading term. Usually a symptom implies that someone is sick, or that his or her body is not functioning properly. Trauma-based symptoms, however, are the body and mind's way of coping the best it can. As uncomfortable and distressing as these symptoms can be, they are actually a signal of health and healing, rather than of dysfunction and illness.

For example, when we have a cut or burn on our skin, the body creates a scab to begin healing it. Scabs are ugly, itchy, and do not look like healthy skin. If we didn't know what a scab was, we might conclude the skin is diseased. In the same way, trauma-related symptoms may look ugly or make the survivor think they are damaged, but in reality it's the body's attempt at healing.

In this chapter I will outline the most common trauma-related effects that survivors experience. I will also try to re-frame these effects as a natural and protective response to a very abnormal situation. The effects of trauma are the body and brain's attempts to re-regulate themselves. In the wake of trauma your nervous system tries to integrate the event and keep you safe from future danger. Unfortunately these efforts interrupt our lives in an upsetting way and are difficult to understand. I will describe many common effects of trauma, but it's important to remember that responses to trauma are individualized and varied.

In the next chapter I will outline some common psychological disorders that are related to trauma. Disorders are simply constellations of different symptoms. Therapists use disorders as a framework for understanding how to treat a patient or client. If it's helpful for you to identify with a disorder in order conceptualize your own struggles, then use that term. If it's more useful to identify with the specific symptoms you experience, that's fine as well.

Common Trauma-related Effects

Re-experiencing the trauma

Re-experiencing means that survivors live their trauma again and again in an intrusive way. Re-experiencing can take the form of flashbacks, nightmares, images, words, and physiological reactions. By saying these effects are intrusive, I mean that they are unintentional. You are not meaning to think about the trauma or conjure up any aspect of it, and yet it pops up. Most often, re-experiencing happens when there is a trigger in the environment. A trigger can be anything that reminds you of the trauma. It could be an object, a person, a sound, a smell, or even a taste. However, re-experiencing can happen with or without triggers present.

Re-experiencing effects are disturbing because they are unwelcome, unwanted, and seemingly random. Most survivors simply want to forget about the sexual assault and go on with their lives, but it seems like their minds will not let them.

Early research about re-experiencing used the term 'intrusive thought,' but we now know that these intrusive memories are more like sensations, rather than discrete thoughts.[i] Re-experiencing usually consists of small fragments of the trauma that are sensory in nature, rather than having to do with words. It's unlikely that survivors have the discrete thought "I was raped" in an intrusive way. It's more common that survivors experience a very brief visual image of something having to do with the assault or another type of bodily sensation. Research has shown that visual images are the most common type of re-experiencing, followed by physical feelings, then sounds, smells, and tastes.[ii]

Clients have described their intrusive memories to me over the years. I remember one young woman who felt haunted by the memory of her rapist's intense stare and felt those eyes watching her when she was alone or getting dressed. Another middle-aged woman would have the feeling of her chest tightening when she felt trapped or powerless, and she said that this feeling was exactly like the feeling of her abuser's weight on top of her body. A man I once worked with who was abused by his older brother had a strong memory of his brother's cologne. When he would catch a whiff of that cologne or a similar one, he said, "It would put me right back there."

Re-experiencing can also occur even if the survivor has little or no distinct memories of the abuse. This is very common with survivors of childhood sexual abuse, but I have also seen it with adults that have been drugged and then raped, so they have no recollection of the actual event. These re-experiencing effects are often emotions or physical sensations that are connected to the abuse but are not accompanied by a visual image or an actual memory. Researchers call this *affect without recollection*.[iii] This means we experience an intense emotion, but have no memory to go along with it.

What makes re-experiencing so distressing is that these memories and sensations lack a perspective of time. What this means is that there is a sense of "nowness" to re-experiencing that is different than simply recalling something from the past. Non-traumatic memories are accompanied by the awareness that the event happened in the past. We can cast our minds back and conjure a memory, all the while knowing that we are not actually *in* the past. Leading researchers on the subject of re-experiencing put is this way:

> The sensory impressions are re-experienced as
> if they were features of something happening
> right now, rather than aspects of memories
> from the past. Also, the emotions (including
> physical reactions and motor responses)
> accompanying them are the same as those
> experienced at the time. [iv]

Traumatic memories come with a sense of threat and danger that puts you immediately on edge. These intrusions on your mind and body are exhausting, confusing, and difficult to deal with.

Intrusive memories also tend to be repetitive in nature. There may be some small detail from the rape that stays with you. Trauma-related memories are very resistant to change. Even if you acquire new information about the trauma, or think about it in a different way, the original emotions and sensory impressions that were formed during the trauma endure.

Why do survivors of sexual trauma experience intrusive memories and sensations? The answer has to do with how traumatic memories are encoded and recorded in our brains. In Chapter 3 we will discuss trauma memories in more detail. For now, it's important to know that memories of trauma are very different from other types of memories. The main difference is that trauma memories lack connections to time and place. Most memories we have about our lives involve *autonoetic awareness*, which is the sense or experience of the self in the past. We can retrieve a memory about an event, and also recall the particular time and place in which it occurred. This kind of memory is called an *episodic memory*, since it relates to a particular episode in our lives.[v]

By contrast, trauma-related memories lack the time perspective that other memories have. They seem to be on their own island, so to speak, without the context that would normally place them in the past. Since there are no time or place cues, we react as if it is still happening. These memories act as cues of threat, and that's why the survivor will often panic or feel anxiety when re-experiencing occurs. And since they exist on their own island, it's difficult to integrate new information about these memories. As stated earlier, intrusive memories are very resistant to change or updating as we learn new information.

So what can be good about re-experiencing?

It's understandable for re-experiencing effects to be distressing, confusing, and to make life difficult. Re-experiencing, however, is also one way in which you are already healing. Re-experiencing is the brain and body's way of forcing you to deal with and understand what happened to you.

As I mentioned in Chapter 1, we are natural meaning-makers. Things happen in our lives and we file them away in their appropriate spots. This is how our memory works, like a giant (and very intricate) filling system. If something new or very odd happens to us, we need to create a brand new "file" for that incident. For example, I remember the first teacher I had that I perceived as mean. This was in elementary school, and all of the teachers I had experienced before her were, in my perception, very nice. My "file" for what a teacher was included a stereotype of a very nice man or woman. When I got this "mean" teacher, I needed to create a new file, or stretch my existing "teacher file" to accommodate a new experience.

We are not born with a file for trauma. Especially sexual trauma, which is devastating in a way that other trauma, such as a car accident or a fire, is not. When a sexual assault happens, it has no place to land, no "file" for it to rest in. Instead we shove it in anywhere we can and try desperately to close the drawer. This is understandable and it's how we try to cope. Unfortunately, the trauma pops right back out again, and will continue to do so, until we create a new trauma file for it to rest in.

This memory wants to be put into the context of our lives. It wants to be understood and examined. This is usually the exact opposite of what we want to do, since this memory is upsetting and very difficult. The intrusive nature of these memories is what forces us to look at it, consider it, grieve over it, and finally put it away.

This is why it's very important in trauma therapy to discuss the actual sexual assault. In all but the most vulnerable survivors, it's helpful to talk about what happened. Of course, a trauma specialist will make sure that the survivor has tools to cope and self-regulate before doing this. As you talk about what happened and allow yourself to get in touch with your emotions, the re-experiencing slowly stops. It may be hard to see right now, especially if you are in the throws of re-experiencing, but talking is transformative. I see it happen again and again with my courageous clients. If these memories were not popping out at us, we'd probably never get around to talking about them, and thus the healing would not happen.

Rumination

Rumination is a trauma effect that is similar to re-experiencing. In rumination, the survivor turns the event over and over, thinking and re-thinking. It's also intrusive in the sense that it's very difficult to get the assault off your mind. What makes rumination different from re-experiencing is that rather than having a visual image or physical sensation pop into your awareness, rumination involves discrete, language-based thoughts. Ruminative thoughts about sexual assault are usually evaluative, meaning that we think to ourselves in order to try and understand what happened. Usually these thoughts evaluate how we acted during the assault, and often this leads to guilt and self-blame.

When someone is stuck in rumination, their thoughts might run like this:

I shouldn't have gone to that bar or drank so much. That's why I was raped. I need to be careful in the future. I hope no one knows about what happened. What was it that he looked like? I can't really remember. Should I tell someone? What if they don't believe me? Or just tell me I shouldn't have put myself in that situation? I need to watch what I drink in the future...

Or this:

I'm only able to remember bits and pieces of what happened. It all seems so fuzzy, like a dream. And it was so long ago; I was just a kid. What if this never even happened, like I made it all up? Why would I have all of these effects then? Am I just crazy? I should have told an adult. I should have stopped it. I wonder how my teacher would have reacted? I wonder if anyone else in my family suspected? Why did this happen to me?

Or this:

Why do I feel so bad about last week? The date went okay, but I guess he was a little pushy. Why do I feel so sad and scared? I really tried to say no. Maybe I didn't really say it. I don't really remember. It all happened so fast. I should have stopped him if I really didn't want it. Maybe I did? I'm so confused about it. I wonder what my friends would say? I saw online that it might be rape or date-rape or whatever. But that can't possibly be right. It wasn't like he had a gun or anything. I should really just forget it and be more careful in the future...

As you can see, rumination has a circular quality. One survivor likened rumination to "chewing the cud" like a cow. She was simply turning these thoughts over and over and not really digesting anything. Rumination can feel like a low hum in the background of your life. It's a constant reminder of the assault. Even though it's on your mind, you don't feel like clarity is any closer.

Since sexual trauma carries a stigma in our society, most people don't report it, and, as a result, survivors are left alone with their thoughts. With no one to discuss them with, they simply bounce around the mind with nowhere to rest.

So what can be good about rumination?

Rumination functions like re-experiencing. Survivors ruminate about their assault because they are not quite sure how to think about it. There is no script for sexual assault in their lives, and it lacks context or understanding. Rumination is the mind's way of bringing up the subject and forcing the survivor to think about it. Hopefully, this thinking will lead the survivor to talk with someone about their experience, or do some research about sexual assault. Through this talking and learning, rumination transforms into narrative.

Creating a narrative is an important step in the healing process. A narrative is simply a story, and our personal narrative is the story we tell ourselves about our life. When rape or molestation happens, it does not easily fit into the rest of our life story. It takes some work, and some learning, to really get our minds around sexual trauma. It needs context and explanation. Simply understanding the myths and facts about sexual assault and naming what happened is a great start to creating an authentic narrative.

In working with my clients I am always helping them create their narrative. We honor and respect their real emotional pain and introduce reality-checks when we need them in order to put self-blaming thoughts in their proper context. We also struggle together with questions about why people assault others, and why bad things happen to good people.

Through this work, a narrative emerges that looks very different from the disorganized and guilt-laden thoughts of rumination. This narrative includes facts rather than myths, inserts compassion and reality where there used to be guilt and shame, and weaves the assault into the larger narrative of the survivor's life. The trauma moves from "the only thing I can think about" to "something really bad happened, and it still bothers me at times." Like a horse slowly taking off blinders, a survivor has a broader view of their experiences.

Creating a narrative also dovetails into the file metaphor we explored previously. The theme is that the trauma needs context and a special psychological space to rest in. Creating that context is hard emotional work. That hard work would probably not happen if we simply ignored our trauma. Rumination is the mind's way of reminding us. It gently (and sometimes not-so-gently) requests our attention. It's saying, "There's something over here that needs to be processed. It's important. Don't ignore it."

Hyperarousal

Hyperarousal is a very common trauma effect. Hyperarousal refers to the arousal of the nervous system. It feels like you are "on edge" all of the time. When we are in danger, our nervous system automatically kicks up a notch. In trauma survivors, it seems that our alarm bells are always going off.

Hyperarousal includes:

- Feeling jittery
- Startling easily
- Being jumpy
- Constantly scanning the environment for danger (also called hypervigilance)
- Being very aware of exits and ways to escape
- Feeling anxious
- Having difficulty sleeping (including not being able to fall asleep and not being able to stay asleep)
- Difficulty eating/low appetite
- Having trouble settling down
- Feeling threatened
- Never feeling safe, even at home
- Easily feeling over-stimulated or frazzled

- Difficulty concentrating
- Physiological problems such as headaches, stomachaches, and nausea

Hyperarousal also refers to our reactivity. People who suffer trauma tend to be more reactive than others, meaning their reactions to stressors are more extreme. If others say to you, "You're over-reacting," this is a reflection of increased reactivity. I like to explain reactivity with a metaphor. Imagine that you have a bucket, and all of the stress in your life is the water in that bucket. You're able to hold a certain amount of water (or stress). But when there is too much, your bucket overflows, and the stress shows on the outside as the water runs over the top and down the sides.

For survivors of sexual assault, their buckets are very close to full on a daily basis. That's the result of holding all the stress of the assault itself and living with the effects of trauma. So when everyday stressors come along, it's more likely that their bucket will overflow. It may seem to the people around you that you are over-reacting or overly sensitive, but the fact is that you are already carrying so much in your system that you are bound to "overflow" at times.

So what can be good about hyperarousal?

Hyperarousal can be distracting and distressing. Being on high alert all of the time is also very exhausting. These effects, however, are your way of staying safe. Your body and mind are aware that you were violated and attacked in a very intrusive way. It wants to make sure that will not happen again. It's a normal reaction to an abnormal situation.

Keeping you at "high alert status" does make you more aware of any danger in your environment. Your system is essentially widening the net it uses to catch anything around you that may be a threat. The downside to this strategy is that many benign things get caught in the net and set off a physiological reaction intended to make you prepared for danger. Since there is no actual danger to react to, your body and mind are left like a prizefighter that got hyped up for a match and no one showed up. There is a lot of restless and directionless energy bounding around inside of you.

Hyperarousal effects are meant to be protective and are outside of conscious control. However hyperarousal is manifesting for you, know that you cannot control it. Recognize that these effects are meant to help you, even if your mind is currently misfiring in the wake of the trauma. In Chapter 8 we will discuss coping skills which are helpful for hyperarousal.

Avoidance

Avoidance is the natural successor to re-experiencing and hyperarousal. Avoidance is the process of evading any trauma-related material. When we are stuck in avoidance, we try to prevent uncomfortable thoughts or feelings from manifesting. If they do pop up, we recoil and beat a hasty retreat. There are three main types of avoidance: emotional, cognitive, and behavioral.

Emotional avoidance is internal; it's the purposeful avoidance of feelings related to the trauma. For example, if you notice sadness come up related to the trauma and think to yourself, "Don't go there" or "Don't be sad" or "I'm going to just ignore that feeling." You may find yourself doing something in order to avoid experiencing you sadness, such as distracting yourself. Emotional avoidance is very understandable. No one feels good about sexual trauma. It is connected to uncomfortable emotions like sadness, shame, guilt, anger, and disgust. It makes sense that no one wants to feel these things. The re-experiencing effects we discussed earlier lead very naturally into avoidance. Re-experiencing brings them up; avoidance tries to shut them down.

The second type of avoidance is *cognitive avoidance*. The term *cognitive* in psychology refers to language-based thought. Cognitive avoidance is the purposeful stopping or re-directing of thoughts about the rape or sexual abuse. Again, re-experiencing and rumination bring to mind thoughts about the rape, and you try to avoid them in different ways. You may simply tell yourself "Stop" or label all those thoughts as dangerous or unhelpful. You may try to distract yourself. Any way in which you try to avoid certain thoughts or lines of thought is cognitive avoidance.

The third type of avoidance is *behavioral avoidance*. As opposed to both cognitive and emotional avoidance, which are internal, behavioral avoidance is external. This type of avoidance refers to actions. Any action or behavior that is intended to help us steer clear of reminders of the trauma can be labeled as behavioral avoidance. This could mean avoiding certain places, such as where the assault itself occurred or places that remind you of the assault. It could mean avoiding certain activities. It could also manifest as avoiding certain people that are connected to the assault in some way.

One particularly difficult way behavioral avoidance manifests is within intimate relationships. It's often very difficult for a survivor to be sexual with a partner, or even with him or herself. Sexual effects for survivors can include:

- Low or no sexual desire
- Feeling very anxious or afraid of having sex
- Having intrusive memories or flashbacks during sex
- Unsure about sexual boundaries

- Inability to orgasm
- Inability to obtain or maintain an erection (for males)
- Unwanted thoughts or fantasies about the abuse or the perpetrator

All of these experiences are very common and are a very understandable reaction to sexual trauma. Unfortunately, survivors bear the burden of re-negotiating their own sexuality with both themselves and their partners. This can be a long and difficult process. It helps to be patient and compassionate with yourself and your partner. Professional sex therapy can also be very helpful for individuals and couples navigating this issue.

Numbing

Numbing is closely related to avoidance; it's how we avoid uncomfortable emotions. Numbing after a trauma refers to feeling emotionally "numb," which means feeling no emotions at all. Although numbing lets us opt out of difficult emotions like sadness and anger, it also makes it difficult to be in touch with positive emotions like happiness and joy. Numbing also refers to difficulty with expressing emotions outwardly. Survivors may appear blank or neutral, neither sad nor happy. They may also appear disconnected from their own emotions, even as they are trying to express them. For example, a survivor may be laughing with you over a joke, but their laughter appears hollow or forced. They may sit in a movie that would normally make them cry but show no sadness.

Numbing is an understandable response to the flood of emotions that come rushing in after a rape. Sometimes numbing is purposeful. You numb yourself for fear of being mired in emotions that are frightening or exhausting. Sometimes numbing is more automatic and occurs beneath the level of awareness. In this case, you simply become overwhelmed with all the emotions, and you shut down. Shutting down is a protective defensive move for your nervous system. It gives your system a period of time to gather itself, similar to how a computer will shut itself down before overheating and damaging its circuits.

So what can be good about avoidance and numbing?

Both avoidance and numbing have one function: to help you re-regulate by having a breather. Just as re-experiencing and rumination bring up aspects of the trauma for you to deal with, avoidance and numbing can kick in so that you don't become completely overwhelmed and unable to function. Both avoidance and numbing are, at their cores, defensive mechanisms that act as a fail-safe. Both allow you to shut out the trauma for a time at the emotional, physical, and behavioral levels.

Avoidance/numbing and re-experiencing/rumination are responsive to each other, and try to balance each other out. Research studies have shown that these two constructs are significantly correlated to each other in rape victims.[vi] However, since they are each extreme compared to our regular day-to-day experiences, the survivor often feels like they are pulled from one polar opposite to another. In one moment they are immersed in trauma memories and flooded with emotions. In the next, they feel numb and push trauma-related thoughts out of their minds. This awkward dance is disruptive distressing and confusing.

Trauma work usually involves trying to find a balance between flooding and avoidance. This must be done in a safe space and at your own pace. When I work with clients I help them get in touch with the trauma experience in a safe way, so that it does not become overwhelming and lead to shutting down or total avoidance. I also take pains to help survivors use avoidance in a mindful way, such as when they really need a break from the trauma effects or do not feel stable enough to let in thoughts or feelings about the trauma.

Finding this balance is a difficult, but doable, process. I have found that an understanding of both sides of the roller-coaster is helpful. Seeing that both re-experiencing/rumination and avoidance/numbing are meant to be helpful to your body and brain can make the process more tolerable.

Dissociation

Dissociation is a psychological term meaning the ability to "tune out" or to mentally leave the present moment. Everyone dissociates to some degree or another, usually in a mild form. Daydreaming during math class is one example of mild dissociation; going on "auto-pilot" while driving home from work is another. Dissociation is the mind's natural ability to project our mental selves into a different time or place. This usually happens subconsciously; our minds just drift away when we are bored, preoccupied, or simply don't need our full attention to complete a task.

Although mild dissociation is very normal and usually harmless, trauma-related dissociation is a stronger type of "checking out." During a rape or an episode of sexual abuse, dissociation occurs because it's too psychologically overwhelming to be in that present moment. We simply can't take it in and so our mind does us a favor by checking out. In this way, dissociation is another type of fail-safe mechanism to avoid being overwhelmed.

Dissociation during trauma can take many forms. Some survivors cannot remember some or all aspects of the trauma. Some survivors can recall the trauma, but they feel disconnected from it, as if they were not fully in their body.

Still others have the sensation that the trauma somehow happened to someone else, even if they intellectually grasp that they were the one assaulted. It's also very common for survivors to feel as if they are watching the event happen from outside their body when they remember the assault. I recall one particular client who was abused as a child by her uncle. She said that she remembered the assaults, but felt as if "I had floated up to the ceiling, and was looking down from there...I felt safer up there, as if he couldn't really touch me because I wasn't down there with him; I was up above him. I remember feeling as if I could crawl up into the cracks in the ceiling and watch from a safe distance."

After the trauma, dissociation effects can continue. Survivors often have difficulty connecting to their bodies. One survivor I worked with described herself as a "walking head" because she had felt disconnected from her body since childhood. For survivors of sexual trauma, the body can be a place fraught with fears, anxieties, and unresolved issues. The body itself may have been labeled as bad or blamed for the abuse, so it makes sense that there is a disconnect. This disconnection from the body can range from complete separation, as in the feeling of watching your own actions from afar, or a milder feeling of being vaguely ungrounded or without a core or center.

More extreme kinds of dissociation can also happen. Some survivors feel as if they check out often and lose periods of time. They may feel as if they are two different people, and they take turns being in control of the body.

So what can be good about dissociation?

When we consider dissociation, we need to keep in mind that it serves a very important function. During a traumatic event like a sexual assault, dissociation is often the wisest course of action. We need to be elsewhere in order to psychologically survive that moment. Dissociation is a survival mechanism, and one we should be grateful for. The dissociative response to trauma operates below our awareness, and so it is not a choice; it simply happens. Dissociation occurs when we deeply realize that we cannot control our situation, that something is happening to us that we cannot stop. So our mind does us a favor by going elsewhere, if only for a time, in order to spare us that horrible reality.

Dissociation does of course have its downsides. It can breed uncertainty and confusion about the event itself. It can leave us feeling disconnected from our bodies. We can have difficulty being in the present moment. It can feel very disruptive when a traumatic experience from the past comes roaring back in full detail, especially when it has been obscured by dissociation for a long time.

I firmly believe that dissociation keeps traumatic events at bay until we have the resources to deal with them. That is why events from the past may be repressed entirely, seemingly forgotten, or they may appear hazy to us. Sometimes past trauma can simply appear strange rather than traumatic, and not trigger any emotional reaction in us. Trauma can lie dormant for days, months, or even years. This has to do with dissociation and our own inner wisdom about our readiness to cope with the reality of our trauma. If a past trauma has re-surfaced for you, you may feel overwhelmed and not sure where to begin in coping. However, the very fact of its arrival in the forefront of your mind is a signal that you are resilient enough to heal.

Relationship Problems

Survivors of sexual assault and molestation often have difficulty with relationships. When your most intimate and vulnerable boundaries are severely violated, it's understandable to feel awkward or unsure in relationships. This can occur on all levels, such as with friendships, co-workers, family members, and intimate partners.

Survivors often feel that they are pulled between two extremes: wanting connection and being afraid of connection.

Sometimes people alternate between wanting to be very social and have others around them, and wanting to be alone and feeling safe in isolation. This external back-and-forth mirrors the internal struggle of not knowing what feels safe. It's painful for survivors to be unsure of their own boundaries with others. It's difficult to deeply want connection and intimacy, and, at the same time, to be afraid of it.

It's common to see these struggles within intimate relationships. Survivors may act either overly sexual, or shut down sexual behavior entirely. They may oscillate between the two. At some point after the rape, some survivors will seek out a sexual partner in order to "prove" they can still be sexual, and that they are in control of their sexual lives. At other times, those same survivors are so afraid of being triggered during sex that they will try to avoid it. It's difficult to negotiate sexuality after sexual trauma and to arrive at a place that is both genuine and safe. When consulted by couples about intimate issues, I always encourage open communication and a lot of patience as both partners navigate the relationship. Couples therapy with a professional who specializes in trauma issues is always a helpful option.

Survivors of childhood sexual abuse tend to struggle more with relationships than survivors of an adult sexual assault. Children are programmed to trust their elders and sexual abuse is a deep betrayal of that trust. The perpetrator of childhood sexual abuse is likely to be an adult that is known and trusted. It may be a family member, a friend of the family, a babysitter, a teacher, or a coach. The common thread is that the perpetrator is usually an important person in that child's life. Furthermore, the child is likely to be in some way dependent on that adult. To be abused by someone whom you expect to protect and nurture you is a very deep wound.

Sexual abuse early in life disrupts the natural progression of emotional and relational development. As we develop, we must encounter and master several interpersonal skills. We develop our autonomy, our initiative, our unique identity, and our individual competencies. Finally, after establishing ourselves as separate individuals, we need to learn to connect with others in a way that does not disrupt our core identity. We learn to be in relationships but not to automatically take on others' thoughts, feelings, or opinions.

The tasks of identity development and keeping boundaries in relationships are difficult for survivors of sexual assault, and especially so for those abused during childhood. Being used against your wishes, solely for another person's pleasure, does not lend itself to developing autonomy. Survivors may only see themselves through others' eyes; they view their value as what they can do for others, rather than seeing their own intrinsic value as individuals. They often act like "people-pleasers" and go out of their way to fit in. They are described as givers and caretakers, often thinking of others' needs before their own.

For this reason, survivors often struggle with boundaries in relationships, and have a weak sense of self. Judith Herman, in her landmark book *Trauma and Recovery,* puts it this way:

> Traumatic events violate the autonomy of the person at the level of basic bodily integrity. The body is invaded, injured, defiled. Control over bodily functions is often lost…this loss of control is often recounted as the most humiliating aspect of the trauma. Furthermore, at the moment of the trauma, almost by definition, the individual's point of view counts for nothing. In rape, for example, the purpose of the attack is precisely to demonstrate contempt for the victim's autonomy and dignity. The traumatic event thus destroys the belief that one can *be oneself* in relation to others.[vii] (Emphasis in original)

Survivors have to balance the desire for connection with the fear of losing a sense of identity. We'll discuss identity problems specifically a bit later in this chapter. For now, it suffices to say that it is very difficult for survivors to genuinely be themselves in relationships and to trust that others will respect them. It's hard to let your guard down, to let others in. Not only is there the fear of being re-victimized, there is the fear of being rejected if others know about the trauma in your life and how it effects you today. There is the possibility of losing yourself in the relationship, and not knowing how to set boundaries. Clients often share with me their struggle to trust, even if they do want to be vulnerable and connect to others.

So what can be good about relationship problems?

Like many trauma effects, relationship problems can be linked to a survival mechanism. Your mind recognizes that someone close to you attacked you, and so it gives signals to be wary of others. You avoid vulnerability in order to be safe. Your mind widens the criteria for danger in relationships. On some level, we all risk being rejected or being taken advantage of in relationships. When we let others in, we are trusting that we will be treated with respect and compassion. For survivors, this natural hesitation is heightened. Our minds would rather mistake a safe person for a dangerous one than let a dangerous person get close.

Recognizing that our unconscious mind has good intentions does not, of course, make relationship problems any less distressing. However, understanding where these problems stem from can lead us to be more compassionate and patient with ourselves. We are reminded of who is safe in our lives, and gently challenge ourselves to open up and be vulnerable.

A Note to Loved Ones

Chapter 11 is devoted completely to exploring the experience of loved ones of sexual assault survivors, but I'd like to make a few notes here as well. If you are a loved one of a survivor, you may be puzzled and frustrated at times with the survivor's behavior. You may not know what to do or say. You may inadvertently tread on some sensitive ground. You may be puzzled by your loved one's reactions to your attempts at connection. I've run many workshops for loved ones of survivors and I have heard their frustration and confusion.

To the loved ones I want to emphasize how much your support means to the survivors in your life. Even if your friend, partner, or relative does not always show it, your presence means the world. Here are some helpful tips for loved ones:

- Be patient. Healing takes a long time.
- Celebrate small steps towards healing.

- Ask what you can specifically do to help.
- Don't treat the survivor like they are fragile or broken, but be sensitive to their needs.
- Be open to talking about the assault, but don't force them.
- Don't pry for details.
- Be clear about your own needs.
- If the survivor is truly over-reacting or being hurtful towards you, let them know in a gentle way.
- Encourage them to engage in activities they enjoy.
- If you are in a sexual relationship, take it slow and practice open communication about what feels good and safe.
- Ask them before touching, even if you just want to give them a hug.

This list is by no means exhaustive, and does not begin to address all the specific needs of loved ones. Rape does not only hurt one person; it hurts many. You, as a loved one, are entitled to all of your feelings about what happened. Most often, loved ones of survivors share with me their anger, disbelief, guilt, and insecurities. They are full of rage that someone hurt their friend, spouse, or family member. They are often in shock when they first learn of the assault, and even afterwards they often feel disbelief. Sexual assault brings up guilt for many loved ones; they believe that they somehow should have protected them (even if they did not know them at the time).

Partners of survivors have also shared with me their insecurities about the assault. They wonder if they can really please their partner, or if they will ever have a "normal" sexual relationship. They may hold back from communicating their own sexual needs for fear of overwhelming their partner or making them uncomfortable.

You are entitled to all of your feelings and reactions about the attack on your loved one. It's important to honor these feelings and process them, so that the survivor does not take them on. Getting professional help can be a good idea, or seeking out a group or workshop aimed at the loved ones of survivors of sexual assault.

Identity problems

Closely related to the problems in relationships that we just discussed are the identity problems many survivors struggle with. Identity problems can be seen as a problem in our relationship with ourselves. When a rape occurs, or a childhood sexual assault comes to our attention, it throws off our image of who we are.

Just like the myths about sexual assault that we explored earlier, we all have stereotypes about survivors of sexual assault. Take a moment to think about what a stereotypical survivor looks like to you. Is this person a woman? Is she young or old? Does she appear unstable? Have mental health problems? Can she hold down a job? Is she married? A mother? A well-respected person? Does she have close relationships?

We all have in our minds an image of what a rape survivor looks like. Then it happens to you, and all of the sudden you need to integrate your own self-image with the fact that you are now a survivor of sexual assault. Most often the reflections I hear from survivors is that they feel like they've lost a basic sense of who they are. They used to feel in control of their lives, and now they feel out of control. They used to rarely show their emotions, and now they have crying spells seemingly out of nowhere. They used to be fun, but now they are sad most of the time. They used to be mellow, and now they feel like a walking bunch of nerves.

It's understandable that sexual assault sends us reeling. All of the trauma effects we have been exploring do not reflect our natural ways of thinking, feeling, and behaving. Almost every survivor I have worked with has described a feeling of "going crazy" or "losing it" when they describe trauma effects. In the immediate aftermath of a rape, or when buried memories of childhood assault roar back into the present, we can feel as if our core self has been hijacked. All we see, hear and think about is the assault, and there is room for little else. We feel not as if the assault happened *to* us, but rather we feel that we *are* our trauma. When trauma is everything we can see, feel, or think about (because our mind is trying to force us to examine it), it's easy to identify with it.

As trauma effects subside, through the passage of time and usually through very hard work in therapy, we still have to work out a self-image that includes the assault. There is no doubt that experiencing sexual molestation as a child or rape as an adult changes us in irreversible ways. It's quite a task to integrate our new ways of being in the world.

The key to progress in this area is being flexible with our self-images and letting go of stereotypes. If we can hold two seemingly contradictory ideas at once, we can expand our identity to include all of our reality. For example, you can recognize your own strength while also holding the fact that you were victimized and helpless at a certain moment. Or by honoring your very valid anger toward the perpetrator as well as honoring the ways in which you are loving to friends and family. Work towards acceptance of both your trauma and your core value. Refuse to accept that you are not a worthy and good person just because someone treated you like you weren't.

Spiritual Problems

We have been exploring the unique challenges with identity that survivors face. Beyond this, the survivor has to grapple with the existential issues that are inherent in the case of sexual assault. Questions like: *Why me? Why do bad things happen to good people? Why do some people victimize others? Was the perpetrator evil, or simply misguided? Why would God, or a Higher Being, allow this to happen? Is there any purpose to my suffering?*

Whether we consider ourselves spiritual or religious, we all hold a basic framework for how the world works and why things happen the way they do. When a trauma occurs, our worldview can be entirely upended. Even if we previously understood that tragic things could happen to us in theory, actually experiencing a horrible tragedy challenges us to re-think our views. It's very unsettling to find the groundwork we had laid through thought, reason, and spiritual learning shift wildly beneath our feet.

Every survivor's journey toward peace around the above questions is unique. This path might include organized religion, a spiritual practice, or a rational approach. I believe all are valid, and whichever path feels right to you is the one to follow.

So what can be good about identity and spiritual problems?

Many survivors have told me that, although they would never wish something like a sexual assault on their worst enemy, they can see how they have grown through the process of healing. I think trauma forces us to grow in unique ways. If we were not forced to wrestle with questions of worldview and identity, we might never do so. In the same way that many of the effects of trauma force us to deal with the trauma itself, having a trauma in your life forces you to dig deeper into yourself. The exploration usually leads to a more secure self and a more nuanced and mature view of the world and spirituality.

As you struggle with questions about the nature of evil in the world and why this tragedy happened to you, meaning is created around your experience. In a truly amazing way survivors forge something positive from a negative event. In the midst of your confusion, you will touch your own resiliency. As Paul Tillich, a great moral thinker, put it: "The vitality that can stand in the abyss of meaninglessness is aware of a hidden meaning within the destruction of meaning."[viii] Being able to stand in the face of meaninglessness and form a new narrative is the essence of strength.

Survivors Speak-Vivian, Age 32

My grandfather molested me when I was really young. I have only hazy memories from that time in my life, but I do have very clear memories of the abuse. He would fondle me and touch my private parts. He would coerce me into touching him as well. The abuse stopped when I was about 8 or so, because he died of a heart attack. I remember putting all those memories away because I didn't like to think about them. I never fully forgot them, but they stayed buried for many years.

About two years ago, I began to feel I was going completely crazy. These memories about my grandfather were all of a sudden front and center. I would have nightmares about him, and occasionally I would have flashbacks. It was always about the same event. Although I don't remember having strong emotions at the time it happened, the flashbacks were full of an intense fear and sense of disgust and shame. I found myself thinking about the abuse all of the time. I felt like I saw reminders around me constantly. I began to ask myself a lot of questions about what happened. I had never had these thoughts before, but now I felt like I needed answers.

I always considered myself a strong person. I could roll with the punches and didn't get upset easily. That changed, at least for a time. I cried easily. I was angry. The smallest thing would set me off. I was always irritable, and quite embarrassed about these changes. I didn't feel like myself anymore.

Up until this time I had felt safe in the world. My home was my sanctuary, and I didn't bat an eye when a friend asked me to go out downtown. But when my trauma sprang up again, I felt scared. Even if I couldn't identify anything scary around me, I was always on edge. Once my friend walked up behind me and tapped me on the arm to get my attention. I swear I jumped ten feet in the air and immediately started to cry. I couldn't sleep in my own bed, and took to sleeping downstairs on my couch so I could have my dog near me.

All of this was, of course, really hard to deal with. I didn't really know what was happening to me. Something had to be wrong with me, and I felt intense shame and guilt both about the abuse and because of all this psychological stuff.

I mustered up all of my courage and called a therapist. I worked with her for about a year, and it was really hard work. The first thing we focused on was simply understanding that all of these symptoms were normal. That itself was a big relief. Eventually I was able to see how they were helping me to heal. I quickly learned that healing is painful, but in the midst of working through my trauma, the symptoms began to subside.

Even after I felt normal again, I was left to do even deeper work. I struggled with my faith and my self-concept. In a way, I had to create a new self-image and a new faith. I came to accept that I was not to blame for the abuse I suffered, and that bad people exist in the world. I learned I was stronger than I ever knew, and at the same time more vulnerable. I learned who to share this with, and how.

I hope that any survivor who reads this will know that they are not alone, and they are certainly not crazy. The mind works in strange ways and the path to healing is not a straight one. But it gets better, it really does. In the midst of all the craziness remember that your mind is doing what it needs to do. Start there, and the rest will follow.

Chapter 3: Trauma-Related Disorders

In this chapter we will review some common trauma-related psychological disorders. I want to emphasize that very few survivors fit neatly into these categories. You may find that you resonate with some aspects of one disorder and also aspects of a different one. A disorder is mainly a list of symptoms, and it falls very short of describing the experience of a multi-faceted individual. I include these descriptions in order to give you a vocabulary to use with professional therapists and doctors, as well as a framework in which to think about your own experience. Some survivors find comfort in the fact that there is a name for what they experience. Others look at these disorders as labels that are not useful. Whatever your view, my goal is to empower you through information. All psychological disorders are defined in the *Diagnostic and Statistical Manual of Mental Disorders* (DSM for short) which is published by the American Psychiatric Association.[i] You can usually find a copy of the DSM at your local library in the reference section.

Post-Traumatic Stress Disorder (PTSD)

PTSD was first developed as a way to describe the symptoms of war veterans. The term "shell-shock" was a forerunner to PTSD. Eventually, the diagnosis was applied to survivors of sexual assault because of the presence of common symptoms. To qualify for PTSD, there must be an event (the trauma) in which there was actual or perceived threat to the physical integrity of the victim, including injury or death. In addition, the victim must respond to this threat with intense fear, helplessness, or horror. Sexual assault fits here because there is always a threat to bodily integrity. In other words, sexual assault equates to a breach of your boundaries. Even if you do not remember having a strong emotional response at the time of the assault, as is the case with dissociation or numbing, the very need to dissociate from the moment implies intense fear and the feeling of being overwhelmed.

There are three main symptoms for PTSD. The first is re-experiencing the traumatic event. This can happen in several ways, as discussed in the previous chapter. The DSM points to remembering the event through intrusive thoughts, dreams, and flashbacks. It also includes physical and emotional reactivity to triggers of the event. The second symptom for PTSD is the persistent avoidance of anything that reminds the victim of the event. This can happen by avoiding people, places, or things that trigger memories of the assault. The inability to remember the event as well as feeling disconnected and numb is also a type of avoidance. The final symptom in PTSD is hyperarousal, which was discussed earlier. The DSM lists specifically the inability to sleep normally, being irritable or having anger outbursts, difficulty concentrating, hypervigilance, and an exaggerated startle response as manifestations of hyperarousal.

If these symptoms appear 6 months or more after the traumatic event, PTSD is labeled as *delayed-onset*. If the symptoms last for less than 3 months it is labeled *acute*. *Chronic* PTSD refers to symptoms lasting more than 3 months.

PTSD is by far the most common diagnosis for survivors of sexual assault. PTSD sounds like a very serious diagnosis, and it certainly is. However, PTSD is very treatable. There are very good psychological methods for treating PTSD. Studies have shown that after treatment, 67% of people have improved so much that they no longer meet the criteria for PTSD.[ii] That is a very impressive recovery rate, especially compared to other types of mental illness. Depression, for example, has about a 50% recovery rate within 6 months, with declining rates of recovery after that.[iiiiv] PTSD is considered to be one of the most treatable mental issues. I believe this is because people are naturally very resilient, and that the PTSD symptoms are predictable and understandable reactions to abnormal events, rather than a reflection of an intrinsic underlying difficulty.

Complex Post-Traumatic Stress Disorder

Complex PTSD is a new diagnosis that is not yet officially in the DSM; it is still being studied and evaluated by researchers. Judith Herman first defined complex PTSD in 1992.[v] Her work with survivors of prolonged and repeated abuse led her to observe specific symptom clusters that the traditional PTSD diagnosis failed to capture. She pointed out that repeated trauma over a period of time was common in situations of captivity (such as a prisoner of war) or when the victim was under the control of the perpetrator (such as childhood sexual abuse). One specific incident of trauma usually gave rise to the traditional presentation of PTSD, but a period of prolonged trauma that included this kind of control manifested a different constellation of symptoms.

Herman writes that "captivity, which brings the victim into prolonged contact with the perpetrator, creates a special type of relationship, one of coercive control" and that this captivity need not be only physical, but can also be "a combination of physical, economic, social and psychological means (as in the case of religious cult members, battered women, and abused children)."[vi] Therapists working with survivors of childhood sexual abuse had observed for years that there seemed to be a "disguised presentation" in these cases.[vii] The symptoms appeared more complex and manifested in the survivor's personality and their relationships with others. There are also difficulties with self-destructive behaviors and dissociation. There are seven main categories of symptoms for Complex PTSD.

1. Regulation of Mood and Impulses

Survivors of prolonged abuse early in life have difficulty regulating their own emotions. They may appear to swing wildly between opposite ends of the mood spectrum. They don't have that calm baseline that most people have. Emotions seem to have a life of their own, and even if the survivor recognizes that they are overreacting, they cannot control them or calm themselves down.

In addition to the difficulty in regulating emotions (or perhaps because of these difficulties), people with Complex PTSD tend to struggle with self-destructive impulses and behaviors. Examples include self-mutilation such as cutting or burning oneself, pulling out hair, or picking at scabs so they cannot heal. Substance abuse is another manifestation of these impulses. Other kinds of self-destructive behavior that are common are impulsive shopping or unsafe sex. These impulses are a way to numb the self from a constant state of hyperarousal and hypervigilance, or are a way to release the tension survivors feel inside.

2. Alteration in Attention or Consciousness (Dissociation)

People that experience childhood sexual abuse become masters at altering their consciousness. It is a highly useful skill to survive an abusive environment. When living with an unbearable reality, it is understandable that people try to change that reality in their minds. Children will use their powers of imagination to have a vision of loving adults around them. They will compartmentalize parts of their reality to maintain a livable world, keeping the images of abuse separate from their everyday existence.

These skills, developed in an unsafe environment, outlive their usefulness as the child grows into an adult and creates a safe environment. However, the tendency to dissociate remains. One of the main features of Complex PTSD is the existence of dissociation, which has two forms: *depersonalization* and *derealization*. With *depersonalization*, there is a sense of detachment from oneself, both from the body and the mind. It's feeling that you are an outside observer of yourself, watching your life like you watch a movie. In *derealization*, you experience your environment as somehow unreal; your life feels dreamlike, distant, or distorted. Either or both of these effects may be present. It's important to note that these alterations in consciousness happen outside of the effects of substances like drugs or alcohol, and are not due to a medical condition such as seizures.

3. Somatization (Physical Symptoms, or How Your Body Holds the Trauma)

Somatization is the manifestation of physical symptoms from a psychological cause. These symptoms are not fake; they simply can't be explained by physical causes alone. We are all familiar with psychological stress impacting our bodies in different ways. For example, we may feel queasy if we are reprimanded by a boss, or get a stress-induced headache.

For people with Complex PTSD, somatic symptoms might be specific (like nausea) or more diffuse (like body pain). Headaches, digestive problems, and pain in the back, abdomen, or pelvic area are very common.[viii] In women, many gynecological problems such as pain during intercourse or inflammation of the tissue in the uterus may be linked to trauma.[ix] Any somatic symptoms are usually persistent over time and may increase or decrease in reaction to general stress.

Survivors of prolonged abuse have had their bodies intruded upon many times. In addition, their bodily needs were often left unattended. Consequently, in adult life they are vulnerable to concerns about their body's functions. It's also the case that the body expresses what we may not be able to express in thoughts or in words. These symptoms in the body may be the body's way of expressing trauma, or an older marker for trauma that has not resolved.

4. Alterations in Self Perception (Identity)

Being in a coercive and controlling relationship has profound effects on identity. Earlier we discussed identity problems as a general effect of trauma. While the survivor of a single trauma event (like a rape as an adult) may feel like she is not herself, the survivor of chronic trauma may lose the sense that she even *has* a self. The term *self-efficacy* refers to the sense that we can control ourselves and, to an extent, the world around us. Someone with high self-efficacy believes that they can create change in their lives if they wish to. A survivor of chronic abuse with Complex PTSD lacks this sense of power in the world. Since their self-determination was taken away by a powerful other, they carry a view of themselves as powerless. To them, others control their destiny.

Self-efficacy is a key ingredient to the development of a stable sense of identity. To view ourselves as autonomous people with valid opinions and feelings, we need past experiences of being listened to, validated, and given choices. When an abuser takes away our most basic of choices (those choices about our bodies), we grow up without a core identity.

Identity problems in the realm of Complex PTSD manifest as chronic guilt and shame about the self. A pervasive sense of the self being damaged or "dirty" is common. In addition, because a sense of self is unstable, it's difficult to know your true opinions, beliefs, or desires. You don't have a good idea of who you are or how you differ from others. It's also common to adopt others' opinions, emotions, and viewpoints, because you don't have your own.

5. Distorted or Ambivalent View of the Perpetrator.

In cases of Complex PTSD, the perpetrator is in a position of power and has control over the victim. Usually the perpetrator is someone the victims knows and trusts. For a victim of childhood sexual abuse the perpetrator may be a family member, a trusted family friend, a teacher, or a coach. Because of the specific dynamics of this type of abuse, the survivor has contradictory and confusing feelings about the perpetrator. Thinking of the perpetrator as a bad person who victimizes others is not possible if, at one time, you were dependent on that perpetrator for protection, affection, and basic needs.

In order to psychologically survive prolonged sexual abuse, Herman writes that:

> [The survivor must] reject the first
> and most obvious conclusion that something is
> terribly wrong with [the perpetrator]. She will
> go to any lengths to construct an explanation

for her fate that absolves [the perpetrator and other neglectful adults] of all blame and responsibility."[x]

Although these mental gymnastics sound confusing, the alternative is the prospect that the world is a dangerous place in which one cannot count on close adults for safety, support, and nurturance. In a situation of dependence, preserving the relationship with our source of basic needs takes precedence over everything else.

The pull toward the perpetrator leads to ambivalent thoughts and feelings. In other words, survivors feel both connection with and revulsion of the abuser. Adults who abuse children often *groom* them for the abuse. They develop trust and affection first, and then slowly violate boundaries until the victim feels too ashamed to tell anyone. The perpetrator often blames the victim for the abuse, saying that they are playing a game, or that the victim allowed for a lesser boundary violation, and therefore wanted the intimacy to go further. The victim is then left with the horror of the abuse which lives alongside pleasant memories of the perpetrator being nice to them or giving them attention and affection. The relationship between victim and perpetrator is complicated and painful.

Herman notes that this part of Complex PTSD includes a preoccupation with the perpetrator, including thoughts or fantasies of revenge. There is also an attribution of power to the perpetrator, even if the survivor is now an adult and has no contact with the perpetrator. This may manifest as a survivor believing that somehow the perpetrator knows that they are thinking about them or that they are speaking about the abuse. It's common to view the perpetrator in a positive light, to feel paradoxically grateful to them or idealize them in some way for "teaching" the survivor important lessons. Finally, the survivor internalizes the perpetrator's distorted moral framework that justified the abuse, such as by accepting that the perpetrator simply expressed their love in an unorthodox way or that the victim somehow seduced them.

6. Difficulties in Relationships

Many of the relationship difficulties that we outlined as normal trauma effects are also present in Complex PTSD. These include isolation and withdrawal as well as a disruption in intimate relationships. There also may be a repeated search for a rescuer figure, meaning that a survivor may choose romantic partners because they perceive this person as strong and being able to "fix" them. There is persistent distrust of others. In addition, survivors with Complex PTSD have difficulty with self-care in relationships, and may find themselves in abusive or co-dependent relationships. Because they lack a strong sense of self, it's easy for them to lose their sense of identity in a relationship. In these unhealthy relationships it's difficult for survivors to assert themselves and stand up to an abusive partner.

7. Alteration in Systems of Meaning

As discussed earlier, living through sexual abuse forces us to contemplate our worldview and presents us with challenges around creating meaning for our lives and for our suffering. In Complex PTSD, these struggles are all too real. These survivors struggle to find a sustaining worldview or spirituality that meets their needs. They may feel a pervasive sense of despair, hopelessness, or apathy. Often, survivors in this diagnostic category may swing between rejecting all forms of spirituality and clinging desperately to a new faith. They tend to be spiritual seekers, always looking for a way to create meaning in their lives.

Dissociative Disorders

We previously discussed dissociation as a common trauma effect. At the time of the trauma (and occasionally for some time afterward), dissociation is a helpful defense mechanism. It gets us through difficult moments until we have the maturity, tools, and support to cope with our trauma. Sometimes dissociation lingers and impairs our lives and it turns into a disorder. I'll discuss two common dissociative disorders linked to trauma.

Depersonalization Disorder

Depersonalization means a feeling of being detached from yourself, as if the things happening in your life are not really happening to *you*, but to someone else. Everyone has had this experience at one time or another, usually when a very shocking event happens, such as a car accident, or even the positive experience of unexpectedly winning an award. It feels like this can't be happening to us because it's so far from our day-to-day experience. If depersonalization becomes persistent and causes distress, it becomes a Depersonalization Disorder. It's important to note that the depersonalization occurs on its own, not due to using drugs or alcohol.

Dissociative Identity Disorder

Dissociative Identity Disorder (DID) used to be known as Multiple Personality Disorder. This disorder is strongly associated with early childhood trauma and sexual abuse is the most common identifiable cause of DID.[xi] In these cases, the child being abused uses their natural ability to dissociate and use their imagination in order to "split" off alternate personalities. The purpose of this splitting is for escape and to break off the trauma into its constituent parts, rather than being overwhelmed by the whole. It's estimated that DID is present in 1 to 3% of the general population[xii].

The hallmark of the disorder is the presence of at least two separate and distinct personalities, each with their own unique ways of thinking, feeling, and interacting with others. Often these personalities are called "alters," shorthand for "alternate personalities." Alters can be different ages or a different gender than the main personality. Alters usually fully inhabit one way of being in the world. For example, one alter may be angry, and be titled "the mean one." One may be vulnerable or sad. Sometimes one personality presents as a child who has never experienced the abuse and holds the innocence inherent in the survivor. Alters usually play a specific role in the survivor's life or take over certain relational tasks for them. For example, the "mean" personality may deal with confrontation while the vulnerable personality may be present during moments of connection. The number of alters varies between individuals with the disorder, but the average is ten.[xiii]

Often people with DID are unaware of their diagnosis for years. When an alter "takes over," the main personality loses that period of time. This experience is often likened to a blackout from drinking too much alcohol. Signs of DID include:

- Noticing new things in your home that you have no memory of buying (for example, furniture, clothes, jewelry, etc)
- Having things go missing or finding things in different places with no memory of moving them
- "Waking up" in an unfamiliar place, with no memory of how you got there
- Periods of missing time or large blanks in your memory
- Think of yourself as "we" or "us"
- People telling you that you often don't act like yourself
- People telling you things that you have done or said with you having no memory of it
- People talking to you as if they know you, with you having no memory of having met them
- The feeling that there are other people inside of you
- Internally "hearing" voices talk to you

As you can imagine, these different personalities can be very disruptive. However, many people with DID are successful in school and their careers, have families, and generally function well. The splitting usually begins in early childhood, and so the internal multiplicity feels normal. To someone without DID, the experience of having multiple personalities sounds very frightening. To someone with the diagnosis, however, the alters can be comforting and switching between personalities can feel very protective.

Treatment for DID aims to help an individual function better and, hopefully, integrate the alternate personalities into the main personality. If you have a diagnosis of DID or think that you have it, it's important to seek treatment from someone familiar with this distinct issue. A specialist is necessary to accurately assess DID and to treat it.

Generalized Anxiety Disorder (GAD)

When someone says they suffer from anxiety, they are usually referring to Generalized Anxiety Disorder (GAD). GAD is characterized by excessive worry about multiple areas of life. Some amount of worry is normal, especially if we have something that justifies the worry, such as an upcoming bill to be paid or an exam we haven't studied for. The kind of worry that presents in GAD is considered irrational because the subject of worry doesn't justify the anxiety that surrounds it. For example, someone might continually worry that their car might be stolen, even though they live in a safe neighborhood and they have a security system. This kind of worry is also uncontrollable; it's like our mind is on its own track and we can't stop worrying. Individuals with GAD tend to anticipate disaster and have difficulty putting things into perspective. This free-floating anxiety is also accompanied by various physical symptoms such as:

- Periods of difficulty breathing
- Fatigue
- Headaches
- Nausea
- Muscle tension
- Muscle aches
- Difficulty swallowing
- Trembling or twitching
- Bouts of numbness in the hands and feet
- Sweating
- Insomnia
- Hot flashes

Thought-related symptoms of GAD include irritability and difficulty concentrating. These symptoms must persist for at least 6 months in order to qualify for the diagnosis. GAD occurs in 1-5% of adults.[xiv]

Anxiety tends to run in families and some people are predisposed to be anxious. This predisposition to worry may be triggered into GAD by a traumatic event. Research has shown that experiencing an event like a sexual assault triples the risk of developing GAD.[xv] A vulnerability to GAD has also been linked to experiences of not being in control, such as childhood sexual abuse.[xvi]

Panic Disorder

Panic Disorder is a disorder characterized by frequent panic attacks. A panic attack is a sudden and intense surge of fear and anxiety. Panic attacks are scary and unpredictable. Having panic attacks, and worrying about having one, is very disruptive to everyday life. Symptoms of a panic attack include:

- Racing heartbeat
- Difficulty breathing, feeling as if you can't take deep breaths
- Feeling of intense fear
- Lightheadedness or dizziness
- Nausea
- Shakiness or trembling
- Sweating
- Chest pains
- Feeling of choking
- Hot flashes or sudden chills
- Fear that you are "going crazy"

- Feeling that you might die
- Feeling like you are having a heart attack (when no medical condition is present)

These symptoms look like a fight-or-flight response to a threatening situation. However, panic attacks are, by definition, responses that are very out of proportion to any perceived threat. Oftentimes, there is no threat at all. They arise out of nowhere and catch us by surprise. Panic attacks are usually short (less than ten minutes). However, when you in the midst of a panic attack, it can feel like forever. About 15% of people will experience at least one panic attack during their lifetime, while about 1% of people will have panic attacks frequently enough to be diagnosed with panic disorder.[xvii]

Panic disorder may co-occur with another anxiety disorder, or may occur on its own. If no other anxiety disorder is present, someone will be generally relaxed and calm except for when a panic attack strikes. People with panic disorder will worry about having an attack because they are embarrassing. Their panic attacks may cause others around them to worry or over-react. People will also try to avoid any triggers that they link to their attacks.

Treatment for panic disorder usually combines talk therapy and medications. Medications might be taken every day or only during a panic attack. Talk therapy for panic disorder will involve learning more about panic and anxiety, and discovering the thoughts and behaviors that exacerbate or sustain feelings of panic.

Depression

Everyone feels low now and again, usually in response to a loss or disappointment in our lives such as losing a job or ending a relationship. This kind of depression is called situational depression, because it's an understandable response to a life event. Clinical depression, on the other hand, is more prolonged and severe. Signs of clinical depression include:

- Depressed mood for most of the day, every day
- Crying spells
- Low self-esteem
- A decrease in interest in normal activities
- Your mood affects your work and/or your relationships
- Inability to get pleasure from activities you normally enjoy
- A significant increase or decrease in appetite
- Sleeping more than usual or sleeping less than usual
- Low energy and fatigue

- Physical agitation (jittery, inability to sit still)
- Feeling 'slow' in your movements, as though you're moving through sand
- Feelings of worthlessness
- Feeling helpless about changing your life or your mood
- Excessive feelings of guilt
- Difficulty concentrating
- Indecisiveness
- Thinking about suicide or that it would be better "if I weren't here"

If a majority of these symptoms occur for at least two weeks, then the criteria are met for a Major Depressive Episode. Two or more Major Depressive Episodes are required to merit the diagnosis of Major Depressive Disorder. Another disorder related to depression is Dysthymic Disorder, which is characterized by a longer lasting (two years or more) but milder form of depression.

Depression is twice as common in women as in men, but the exact reason for this disparity is unknown.[xviii] Generally, major life stressors (including, of course, sexual assault) are associated with developing depression. One study investigating the link between childhood sexual abuse and adult-onset depression in women found that early abuse significantly increased the likelihood of developing depression. In women who experienced early sexual abuse, 83% were later diagnosed with depression compared to 32% of women who did not experience abuse.[xix] A similar study found the disparity to be 86% to 36%.[xx] In female victims of adult rape, one study showed that 68% of women reported depressive symptoms, with 24% qualifying for severe depression.[xxi]

Depression is like shutting down. When we are depressed, our mood and energy is low. We don't get a thrill out of doing our favorite activity, engaging with our hobbies, or being with our loved ones. The world feels flat and gray. Our eating and sleeping habits are dysregulated. It's understandable that a sexual assault can dysregulate our bodies and lower our mood. Similarly, a history of abuse can lead to a long-standing depression in which our self-esteem is low and sadness is our constant companion.

Like most psychological disorders, the best treatment for depression combines psychotherapy with medications such as anti-depressants or mood stabilizers.

A Note about Disorders

As mentioned at the beginning of this chapter, it's rare for someone to fit neatly into any one of these categories, and many of the symptoms of different disorders overlap. Most survivors reflect the symptoms found in Post-Traumatic Stress Disorder (PTSD). That being said, it's rare to find a survivor of sexual assault who does not struggle with at least some aspect of depression, anxiety, or dissociation. How your mind and body responds to trauma is unique and influenced by many factors. I chose to highlight the disorders that are most commonly associated with trauma, but others that may reflect your experience include eating disorders, obsessive-compulsive disorder, and personality disorders such as borderline personality. Please refer to the DSM or your mental health professional to learn more about these.

Survivors Speak-Noah, Age 36

I was abused by my older brother from age 6 until I was about 12. He was 5 years older than I was, and in his late teens he was arrested for stealing cars and went to jail. Since then he's been in and out of jail, and we don't speak. It wasn't just sexual abuse; he terrorized me. He would beat me up and call me names. He would manipulate me to get what he wanted. And when we were alone he would touch me, and make me touch him. I felt so ashamed. He would tell me that our "games" had to be kept secret, and that if I didn't keep our secret he would tell everyone it was my idea and that I was a pervert. Of course I believed him. I think everyone looks up to their older siblings. They seem to know so much about the world. I assumed he was right. Even if he hadn't threatened me, I think I would have kept quiet out of shame.

It was a really confusing experience. On the one hand, my brother scared me. On the other hand, he was my playmate and friend. He was always protective of me and looked out for me. For a long time I couldn't square these two things in my head.

As I grew up I began to feel haunted by my past. I would have nightmares about my brother. When I tried to date and be intimate with women, I would be triggered and have flashbacks. My inability to get close to anyone made me feel depressed. I always felt anxious when I was dating anyone, afraid I would act strange. Most of the time I just avoided dating and told myself I was happier being alone.

For a long time I avoided going to the house I grew up in. My parents still live in the neighborhood, and being anywhere close to that house would make my whole body tense up. I would feel anxious and nauseous, and so I would make excuses to not go there.

I was always a high-strung sort of person. I had a hard time relaxing, and as time went on I became more and more tense. I had a hard time sleeping and never had an appetite. I would snap at people, and jump if they startled me.

I lived with layers of shame. First, the shame of the sexual abuse and then, on top of it, shame about these problems I had in my life and my emotions. I really thought that I was losing it. I think what kept me from really dealing with my past was the fear of being labeled as crazy. I thought if I ignored my symptoms, they might just go away with time.

One night I was watching a TV show that had a story about a woman that was sexually abused as a child. They said she had PTSD, and I looked it up because it sounded a lot like me. Learning about PTSD, and especially about Complex PTSD, was a huge relief to me. Having a name for it helped me talk to my doctor, who told me about a therapist I could see if I wanted. I put it off for a while, but I finally called. The therapist confirmed that I have PTSD, and also some aspects of Complex PTSD. He really normalized the whole thing, and de-mystified it. It got so that we could even joke about it. If I was having a bad day, I could say that my PTSD was acting up.

I worked with him for a while, and it was very helpful. I did a lot of work on my own too. I read about PTSD and tried out different strategies for dealing with my symptoms. Eventually I hit on some things that worked for me. Eventually I started dating again and when it became serious I was able to tell my girlfriend about my past and explain that sometimes my PTSD comes to visit again, especially if I'm stressed out. She was so understanding and supportive. I think having a name for what I was feeling helped us to talk about it.

Chapter 4: How Trauma Impacts the Brain

When we understand how trauma impacts the brain we can stop blaming ourselves and gain insight into our own process of healing. I remember one client saying to me about the immediate aftermath of her rape: "I'm trying to be shaken, not stirred. I understand this is a big deal, but I really didn't want it to wreak havoc on my mind. Now I feel like I'm shaken, stirred, and whirled all around." In the aftermath of a trauma, we do feel shaken up and stirred around. Our brain has received a big shock, and it responds in the best way it can; our instinctual response to trauma is always survival.

We will first explore how the brain reacts to trauma, and how it becomes dysregulated. Then we will turn to how you can bring balance back to your brain.

On Being Unbalanced: Left Brain/Right Brain

Our brains have two halves, called hemispheres. The size of our brain is roughly equivalent to the both of your fists placed side by side with the thumbs touching each other. You can imagine that the left fist is the left hemisphere, and the right fist is the right hemisphere. The two hemispheres function differently, and this difference comes into play within the realm of trauma.

The left hemisphere is our analytic side. It's responsible for analytic, logical thoughts. It's the processing center that we use to solve problems, make inferences, and draw conclusions. The left brain is activated when we work with math problems or do science experiments. It's also important because it controls language. Almost all of the processing that occurs in the left brain is language-based. Our ability to verbalize our thoughts, feelings, experiences, and reasoning is centered in the left brain.

By contrast, the right hemisphere is our creative side. It's intuitive and is responsible for our "gut feelings" and impulses. The right brain gives us strokes of insight and helps us be creative. It's activated when we play music and make art. The right brain is where our holistic thinking resides, the type of thinking where we grasp the big picture first and work out the details later. For example, we may intuitively know how to interact with a difficult supervisor at work, but it would be a difficult task to explain logically why we would interact this way.

There are two ways that this left/right division impacts the brain during trauma. The first has to do with the confusion between words and actions on the part of a perpetrator. This usually occurs in survivors of childhood sexual abuse, but can occur during an adult sexual assault. When a perpetrator's words do not match his or her actions, the connections between language and feelings become confused. It's not uncommon for a perpetrator to says things like "I love you," "I would never hurt you," or "I know you like this" while abusing or assaulting the victim. Our bodies and minds know that we are being assaulted and intruded upon in a traumatic way, but those words are meant to soothe us. Usually, hearing someone tell us they love us and will keep us safe makes us feel calm and secure. But if these words are paired with sexual violence, our language center (left brain) and our intuition center (right brain) are in conflict.

In this situation it's difficult for us to explain our experience logically, even to ourselves. Our left brain struggles to reason why a person who says that they care can hurt us so badly. Our right brain gets conflicting signals about danger and safety. If this happens repeatedly to a child, their understanding of words like "love," "caring," and "safety" become skewed. Once this child grows up, they may link love with abuse or believe that they can only have a secure relationship if their partner is always pleased sexually. They may distrust others who claim to care about them. It's also common for adults abused as children to use their sexuality as a tool to get attention or affection from others. It's understandable, since they learned as a child that sexual behavior is the only road to caring. This sets the stage for the cycle of re-victimization, which we will cover in more detail in Chapter 6.

How the left and right hemispheres communicate is also implicated in trauma. The two hemispheres are connected by a bridge called the *corpus callosum*. This bridge is a big bundle of nerve cells that transmit messages between the two hemispheres. This bridge keeps the brain in balance, and is crucial to our processing of events. We need both of our hemispheres to form a complete picture of our world and ourselves.

During trauma, however, this bridge gets disrupted. Communication between the left and right hemispheres is temporarily stopped. Like all of the brain's reactions during trauma, this is actually a wise coping mechanism. This disruption in communication lets our brain break up the trauma into pieces, rather than letting in the whole thing at once, which would be overwhelming. Our brain needs to keep us "together" enough in order to survive the trauma and resume some type of normal functioning afterwards. Because the two hemispheres have not communicated during the trauma, however, there is a separation between the "facts" of the trauma (left hemisphere) and our general emotional impressions related to the trauma (right hemisphere). This disharmony between the two processing centers leads to problems in categorization. In Chapter 2 we explored different trauma effects and the fact that our brain does not have a "file" for trauma. This disconnect contributes to that categorization problem. Neuroimaging studies, where researchers can literally look at different brain regions, have shown that prolonged abuse results in a shrinking of this bridge between the two hemispheres.[i]

Researchers have found that when people recall traumatic memories, their right hemispheres show increased activity, while the left hemisphere shows less activity.[ii] This may explain why trauma memories feel dreamlike and are difficult to put into words. The logical/rational side of our brain is not working effectively. By contrast, our intuitive/instinctual side is on overdrive, and this can flood us with all the emotions and physical impressions that are connected to the trauma.

In traumatized individuals, there is an increase in abnormalities in the left hemisphere, while the right hemisphere seems to dominate functioning. Many survivors of sexual assault feel like they lost that side of themselves that was calm, cool, collected, and rational. All of the sudden, they are living on instinct. This is because most processing is going on in the right hemisphere, rather than being balanced between the two sides of the brain.

The Injured Gatekeeper: The Thalamus

The *thalamus* is a relatively small part of the brain, but it has the important role of gatekeeper and traffic-director. The name thalamus derives from the Greek word for "chamber." Almost all the sensory information we take in from our environment is first routed to the thalamus. The only type of information that bypasses the thalamus is our olfactory sense (the sense of smell). Everything else, whether it's sound, taste, touch, or sight, goes directly to the thalamus. The thalamus then directs all of this information to the proper place for more processing. Information from our eyes gets routed to the visual processing areas, which are in the back of the brain. Sound information gets directed to the auditory processing centers, and so on. The thalamus is like a giant switchboard, making sure information gets where it needs to go. Information from our environment is not interpreted or processed in the thalamus. The thalamus sends it to its proper place, and it gets organized there.

Not only does the thalamus direct incoming information, it prioritizes it. The brain registers an enormous amount of sensory input from our environment, but most of it is not very useful for our everyday functioning. For example, we rarely are aware of continuous background noise or the feeling of our clothes on our body. Our brain has effectively tuned these things out so that we can use our precious attention to complete the task before us. If we were constantly aware of all aspects of our environment, we would never be able to function.

So the thalamus is also a screener. It chooses what to send up for higher processing and what to let go. It distills information into a more manageable form. Because it is a screener, it's responsible for turning up or turning down our alertness to certain aspects of our environment. This alertness is call arousal. We learned about hyperarousal as a common trauma effect in Chapter 2. It's hypothesized that, in the case of hyperarousal in trauma survivors, their thalamus is less active than non-survivors. Brain scan studies have shown that the thalamus region in survivors registers less blood flow than control subjects.[iii] It seems that the original trauma disrupted the functioning of the thalamus and it's not working properly. Since it's getting less blood flow, we can assume it's less active and that much more sensory information is getting sent on to other brain regions. The gatekeeper is letting in more than it should. This leads to an overflow of information about the environment, making trauma survivors hyperalert, jumpy, and high-strung.

Hyperarousal is disruptive and uncomfortable, but it's an effect of our brain's ultimate goal of survival. The brain would rather have a false positive than a false negative. That is, it would rather register a non-dangerous object or person than to not be aware of a dangerous object or person. It would rather we react to the stick on the ground as a snake, rather than think a snake is just a stick. It errs on the side of caution and lets in large amounts of information hoping that by widening the net, it may catch some dangerous fish.

The Thalamus as Timekeeper

One hallmark of the experience of sexual assault survivors is the fragments of memory that constitute flashbacks, intrusive thoughts, and nightmares. This is the re-experiencing effect that we learned about in Chapter 2. These fragments are usually sensory in nature, rather than discrete thoughts. Researchers have consistently found dysfunction in the thalamus of trauma survivors, and this dysfunction may be related to re-experiencing.

Since the thalamus prioritizes and organizes information to pass along to the higher processing centers, its dysfunction results in sensory information not getting to the right place, or not being passed along at all. It's in the higher processing centers that sensory input becomes integrated; that is, it gets processed and made sense of. Connections are made between thoughts, feelings, and physical sensations so that we experience an event as an integrated whole. Dysfunction in the thalamus, however, results in our trauma being split off into different parts. So we may experience a feeling of panic with no discernible event to go with it. Or we may have a flashback of seeing the event happen, but without the correlating physical sensations.

Additionally, these sensory fragments are experienced as timeless. When they are recalled, it's like it's actually happening in the present rather than the past. My clients often describe their memories of sexual assault as if those memories were on an island by themselves and not connected to the other memories from that time. This lack of context is due to a dysfunction in the process of *temporal binding,* which happens in the thalamus.

Temporal binding is process of time-stamping memories so that they can be placed in chronological order. This happens because groups of cells in the thalamus can fire at very specific frequencies, resulting in a pattern of oscillation. In other words, certain cells in the thalamus (and other brain regions) fire in a synchronized way. This pattern of firing binds different pieces of our internal and external experience in the time domain. Temporal binding puts things in order so we have a sense of when they occurred relative to our other experiences.

Dysfunction in the thalamus disrupts this process. Without temporal binding individuals who have experienced trauma cannot integrate the trauma into the rest of their memory system. This may account for flashbacks and intrusive memories.[iv] What's more, since the trauma is not bound to the rest of experience, it does not become integrated into the sense of self or our overall life story.

Unregulated Fear: The Amygdala

The *amygdala* is a small brain structure located deep within the temporal lobes of your brain. Those are the lobes that are located just behind your ears. The amygdala plays a key role in processing different emotions, but is chiefly the regulator of fear and anxiety. It's part of the lower brain systems, which are responsible for all our survival reactions and responses. When the amygdala functions normally, it allows for *fear acquisition*, or learning to fear a particular event because of its effect. For example, if we touch a hot stove for the first time and get burned, the amygdala links these two events (touching a hot stove and getting burned), and creates an alarm system based on hot stoves. The next time we are near a hot stove, this alarm goes off, fear is triggered, and we back away.

In trauma survivors the amygdala tends to be hyperresponsive. The fear response is triggered more often than it needs to be. Due to trauma, the amygdala operates on a hair trigger, and this leads to anxiety, panic attacks, and general fearfulness. The fear acquisition is also on overdrive, so anything that reminds us of our trauma can trigger a fear response. When survivors are shown trauma-related photographs, trauma cues, trauma-related words and sounds, and when the survivors recount their experiences, studies show the amygala reacts more intensely than in non-survivors.[v] These exaggerated responses in the amygdala are correlated with the severity of PTSD symptoms.[vi]

The amygdala regulates a fear response, and a fear response is not a single thing, but a complex series of neural and chemical events that gets us ready for danger. It's this fear signal that triggers the fight/flight/freeze response in all animals. It's no wonder that survivors of sexual assault are generally fearful, and are triggered so often. It's important to remember that this fear response operates beneath the level of awareness. We don't need to have a conscious thought about danger in order to react. We are wired to react almost instantaneously. This is what helps us survive. When our amygdala is so responsive, we unconsciously register danger everywhere.

No Checks or Balances: The Medial Prefrontal Cortex

The *medial prefrontal cortex* (MPC) is a brain region well connected to the amygdala in humans and all primates. The MPC is located behind our foreheads and has many functions. One important function that relates to trauma is that of *fear extinction*. Fear extinction is the process of learning *not* to be afraid of something. It's like undoing the fear acquisition. If a fear is acquired, the thing that is feared (like the oven in our example) triggers a fear response as long as it's linked to a negative outcome (like burning our hands). If we encounter the feared object or situation and then nothing bad happens, the process of fear extinction begins. Our brain (specifically the MPC) notes that we can be safe around ovens, and we gradually lose our fear.

The MPC works with the amygdala in a check-and-balance system. The amygdala helps us learn healthy fears of certain things or people, and the MPC works to suppress the fear response once we learn those things are not dangerous, or not always dangerous. The MPC integrates new information about previously feared objects, and reverses fear conditioning so that we can walk around in the world not being afraid all of the time. For example, if I am bitten by a dog then I learn to be afraid of dogs. But I run into dogs all the time, and I see lots of dogs that do not bite me. The MPC notes this and gradually extinguishes my fear of all dogs.

If the MPC is damaged or dysregulated in some way, fear extinction does not occur, and this is the case with survivors of trauma. Our irrational fears persist, and the amygdala runs on hyperdrive with no regulation from the MPC. Imaging studies of the brain show a decreased volume of the MPC in individuals suffering from post-traumatic stress. Other studies have shown that the severity of PTSD symptoms is inversely correlated with the size of the MPC.[vii] That is, the more severe the symptoms, the smaller the MPC. Many studies have shown that the MPC fails to activate for individuals with PTSD, specifically when they are exposed to cues related to their trauma. Overall, there is evidence for malfunction of the MPC in traumatized people on the structural, neurochemical, and functional levels.[viii]

In Recovery: Hitting the Reset Button

When a sexual assault happens, our brain goes into survival mode, which we might also call trauma mode. In an effort to survive our brain keeps us on high alert, looking for danger. It also shuts down the mechanism that suppresses our fear response, resulting in jumpiness and fearfulness. Additionally, we lose the time context for the trauma and react as if it's happening again and again. Many different brain areas and brain processes become dysregulated. It can take some time to hit the reset button and get back to normal functioning.

The good news is that our brains are not static; they are constantly changing, both in response to our environment and in response to internal strategies we can control. The process of change in the brain is called *neuroplasticity*. Our brain is able to move and bend to accommodate our needs.

Since you are in recovery from a trauma, there are certain strategies that are helpful to begin recalibrating your brain. There are also treatments and specific tools that are helpful with this resetting process, which we will discuss in Chapter 9. For now, here are strategies to help heal your traumatized brain.

1. Regulate your body's needs.

Focus on the Big Three: eating, sleeping, and moving. Eat regularly, and eat healthy. The brain is an organ that requires a large amount of calories to function at an optimum level, and functions best on a balanced diet. It's very common for trauma survivors to turn to food for comfort. It's normal to want junk food to numb out, soothe ourselves, or dull emotional pain. Don't cut out your favorite foods from your diet, but do focus on health and on eating foods that help you feel alert and satisfied. If you are struggling at regulating your emotions, it's helpful to think about taking a break from alcohol and caffeine.

The second area to focus on is sleep. Anxiety and hyperarousal often dysregulate sleeping patterns, but you can set yourself up for better sleep. Here are helpful strategies for sleep:

- Have a consistent sleep schedule. Go to bed and wake up around the same time every day.
- Don't watch TV, play with your phone or tablet, or do anything too stimulating while in bed (reading is fine).
- Don't have caffeine after noon.
- Your bed is a place to sleep, so if you lie down and are unable to fall asleep after 30 minutes, get up and do something low-key like reading in another room. When you begin to feel sleepy, return to your bed.
- Take a hot shower to relax before going to bed.
- -Exercise sometime in the evening to make you more ready for rest (even taking a walk can make a difference in your sleep patterns).

The third of the Big Three is exercise. Exercise is extraordinarily helpful with the regulation process. You don't need to run a marathon, you just need to move your body. Exercise promotes the growth of new neurons in the brain, a process known as *neurogenesis*. In addition, exercise triggers a chemical response in the brain that stimulates neuroplasicity, letting the brain change and be flexible.[ix] Exercise is also known to improve mood and boost a sense of well-being. Find a fun activity and aim to do moderate exercise for 30 minutes a day, most days of the week.

2. Relaxation

When our brains are in survival mode, it's very hard to relax. However, staying in a hyperalert state can be self-reinforcing. We need to break this pattern by intentionally relaxing. By doing this, we are signaling to our brain that we are actually not in danger. Over time, our brains can integrate this and gradually move out of survival mode.

Of course, relaxing on command is almost impossible. It may seem counter-intuitive to be intentional about relaxation, but putting relaxation as a priority means we have to be serious about it. If you already know what relaxes you, make time for these things. If you don't know what is relaxing, explore some activities in order to find what works for you. For some, a favorite TV show is relaxing. For others, a massage is the key. Experiment until you find what works for you.

Part of relaxation is avoiding overloading yourself with tasks or activities. Even something fun can feel like a chore if we don't have enough downtime. Make a point to say 'no' to certain things in order to have a manageable schedule.

3. Education

When in recovery from trauma, knowledge is power. When a sexual assault happens, we usually cannot even wrap our minds around what occurred. We feel confused and ambivalent, unable to decide what to think about this horrible event.

It's important to arm yourself with information. The more you know about what is happening with your brain and body, the more compassionate you can be with yourself. Reading this book is a great first step, and I encourage all the survivors I work with to seek out information through books, articles, videos, or the Internet. At the end of this book is a resource list with books, websites, and organizations that support survivors.

4. Activate your logical brain

Most of the dysregulation in the brain due to trauma is in our non-verbal, instinctual, and emotional regions. These regions are in survival mode and during survival we rarely stop to reason out what we are doing. We simply act on instinct. As part of the re-regulation and healing process, you can intentionally activate reasoning centers to link our thoughts, emotions, and behaviors.

Become a curious, but non-judgmental, observer of yourself. Ask yourself, what was I thinking or feeling when I did that? Might I be responding from a place of fear? Are my instincts taking over here? What was the trigger that led to me snapping? Begin to link what you have learned about trauma effects with your behaviors in the moment. The goal here is not to completely control your reactions, because there will still be times that survival-mode will take over, but to begin to stimulate your higher reasoning and become more self-aware.

5. Cultivate your support system

We often get our cues about regulation from others. It seems like emotions are sometimes contagious. If you are around a very anxious person, you may feel anxious yourself. Having calm people around can make us feel calm. If we are alone with our dysregulated brain, it's easy for fear and anxiety to run rampant. Be intentional about seeking out friends and family that have a calming, grounding effect for you. Simply being around another person that is supportive can help reset the brain.

One of the most consistent and predictable connections in the trauma research field is between PTSD symptoms and social support.[x] More social support leads to a decrease in PTSD symptoms. One explanation for this finding is the theory of *stress buffering*.[xi] This model explains that a strong social support network acts as a buffer between an individual and the stressful events in their lives. A corollary to this is the finding that PTSD symptoms themselves lead to an erosion of that much-needed social support.[xii] The social withdrawal, irritability, fearfulness, and anxiety that defines trauma keeps others away, even when the survivor needs them most.

Most survivors I have worked with understandably worry about others' reactions to their experiences. They worry they will be blamed for the abuse, judged, or seen as weak in some way. In my experience, the support people who defy these fears far outnumber the ones who confirm them. You don't need to talk about the sexual assault with your support network, but you do need to make an effort to have them around. If you don't want to share with them exactly what you are struggling with, try simply telling a friend that you are going through a rough time and would appreciate their support. You can look into support groups for sexual assault and abuse in your area to connect with others who really know what you are dealing with. Isolation and withdrawal leads to feelings of aloneness, and no one deserves to go through trauma alone.

Survivors Speak: Melissa, age 35

I have a really stressful job as a lawyer. I work a lot of hours, and over the years I've learned what I need to survive my crazy work week. It took some trial-and-error, especially at the beginning of my career, but eventually I got into a rhythm that worked for me. I was really good about taking care of myself.

Then I was raped. I was on a first date with a man I met online. I had just waded into the world of online dating, hoping to make a connection and find a relationship. Instead I was sexually assaulted. In the aftermath I was knocked off balance and had to find my rhythm all over again.

I am a very intellectual person. Being a lawyer, I'm constantly reading and researching so I can know everything I can about a case. After I was raped I felt like I was going crazy and had no idea what was happening to me. I felt like my brain had been hijacked. I was talking to a good friend and explaining how I felt. She told me, "Melissa, you always feel better if you know what's going on. You should figure out why you feel this way." She was absolutely right. Although I couldn't control my emotions, I could find out what was happening to me.

In learning about how humans react to trauma, I was able to see that I was in survival mode. Even though I returned to my normal life after the rape, my brain was still dealing with the aftershocks. While I couldn't speed up the process the way I wanted to (I wanted it over immediately), I was able to find my feet again.

I took my self-care seriously. I concentrated on all those things I usually did to find balance in my hectic life. Simple things like getting enough rest and sleep. I began to eat regular meals again, and my appetite returned. I worked out my anger at the gym. I began to journal about my day, and was able to find patterns between my emotions and my behaviors. I called my friends to check-in. Some of them knew about the rape, and some didn't. They helped me get out of the house and offered a listening ear. I read some books about sexual assault and trauma.

I began to slowly feel better. I wasn't frightened all the time, and I could think about the rape without losing it. It was a process, but I found out how resilient I really am.

If I could tell other survivors one thing, I would stress the importance of self-care. You need to put yourself first. We all have skills and ways to cope with our already busy lives. I would encourage you to draw on these coping skills. Your whole nervous system was rocked, and it needs time to adjust.

Chapter 5: How Trauma Memory is Different

In this chapter we will explore the nature of trauma memory. Memories of trauma are fundamentally different than other memories. Often, these differences lead to distress for survivors. They wonder, why can't I remember exactly what happened? Why do I feel numb when I put myself back there? Or, conversely, why do I feel these emotions with no memory to match them? Understanding how trauma memory works will help to validate and normalize the unique experience of remembering your assault.

One of the most fundamental activities of the brain is the creation and retrieval of memories. Not only do we rely on our brains to record events, we take it for granted that these events will be woven into a seamless narrative that creates a conscious, continuous, and stable self. Once the disparate bits of memories are integrated in this way, they are never experienced as separate again. Our memories are also influenced by other prior events, future events, and even our mood when we recall them.

Much research has been done to investigate how trauma memories are different than normal memories. We now know that, in a moment of trauma, our memory systems are affected in profound ways that lead to the unique features of trauma memory.

Although we think of our memory system as cohesive whole, we actually have two different memory systems. Under normal circumstances, these two systems work in tandem with each other to form a full memory. *Explicit memories* (sometimes referred to as declarative memories) are memories that can be consciously recalled, such as general facts and knowledge about the world. The explicit memory system is also responsible for recording specific personal experiences and is very language-based. Examples of explicit memories are recalling the capital of Wisconsin, the name of your fifth grade teacher, or what gifts you received on your tenth birthday.

The second memory system is called *implicit memory*. Implicit memories are unconscious memories that we unintentionally pick up from our experiences. These are schemas that we create from doing things over and over. For example, when we learn how to ride a bike, the knowledge of how to move our bodies and balance are stored in implicit memory. Implicit memories also hold our conditioned emotional responses. For example, if I was scared by a clown when I was young, I may feel a twinge of fear whenever I see a clown. It's important to note that the emotional response can exist on its own; I don't need to have an explicit memory of being frightened by a clown when I was young to continue to have this fear response.

In moments of trauma such as a sexual assault, our explicit memory system gets disrupted and goes off-line.[i] Our brains do this as a defensive survival mechanism; it prevents us from completely letting in that awful event. If our explicit memory system was up and running during an assault, it would overwhelm us. While the explicit system is disrupted, the implicit memory system, the one that records emotional responses and bodily sensations, remains untouched.

For survivors of sexual assault, these memories of primal emotions (often fear or shock) and bodily sensations (often of feeling paralyzed or deeply disgusted) are more accessible than a language-based narrative of the event itself. Even if a survivor cannot state in words what happened when, they are haunted by the non-verbal implicit memories. It's also common for one or two particular visual images to be prominent for the survivor, as these visual flashes are non-verbal in nature.

These types of implicit memories are different in several ways from non-traumatic memories. Non-traumatic memories tend to fade over time. By contrast, trauma memories are usually experienced vividly and as if they are happening now.[ii] Non-traumatic memories are also subject to continuous revision as we grow older, gain new perspectives, and integrate new experiences. We can all recall a time we

were very upset as a child, such as when we didn't g
we wanted. We can remember what it felt like in th
to be disappointed, but we also can't help viewing that event
through our adult mind, a mind that has learned to cope
effectively with disappointment and can put that particular
distress in context. Not so with trauma memories.[iii] It's as if
they are an island unto themselves, and even if we grow older,
gain more experiences, and learn about the nature of our
trauma, the memory itself is stubbornly immutable.

The static nature of trauma memories is attributed to
the disruption of the explicit memory system during a
traumatic event. Because our language-based organization
system is down, trauma memories are not fully integrated on a
verbal or symbolic level. This leaves the brain with no choice
but to organize these memories on a sensory or emotional
level. This leads to the nightmares, flashbacks, and bodily
sensations that mark the survivor's experience.

Furthermore, these trauma-based memories are usually
triggered by stress. Research has shown that survivors of
sexual assault are, under normal circumstances, very well-
adjusted.[iv] However, under stress a survivor may feel as if they
are being victimized all over again. Stress is a trigger that leads
to the re-activation of trauma-based bodily sensations,
memories, or behaviors. In other words, because trauma
memories are not integrated in a normal way, they are

triggered by anything that looks remotely like a threat. Put back into that trauma state, people become fearful, hyperalert, and withdraw from others.

Two Sides of the Spectrum: Intrusive Memories and Blank Spots

Not only do survivors struggle with intrusive non-verbal memories, they also have a deficit in the explicit (verbal and fact-based) memories of the assault itself. It's paradoxical that for survivors of trauma, there is both too much memory and too little. Survivors struggle with both the intrusive memories and a blank spot where the explicit memories should be. Many survivors report that they do not remember a large amount of the sexual assault. In cases of childhood sexual abuse, survivors may have no explicit memories for entire years of their childhood.

The brain area that controls most of the explicit memory system is the *hippocampus*. The hippocampus is particularly sensitive to environmental stressors like trauma. It's sensitive because it contains a large amount of receptors for specific stress-related neurochemicals. It's also sensitive because, unlike other brain structures, it continuously undergoes reformatting. By contrast, most other brain structures change and develop until late adolescence, and then their basic structure is set.

The hippocampus is extremely important for memory functioning. It's the first place that explicit memories are stored, and, after a few weeks, it organizes them for long-term storage in other brain areas. When we retrieve a memory (like thinking back to our tenth birthday), it gathers the disparate pieces of memory from around the brain and organizes them. We know that extreme stress such as trauma leads to the dysfunction of the hippocampus. In some cases, it actually shrinks in size. This may account for the memory deficits in survivors of trauma.

Forgetting: The Repression of Trauma Memories

The idea that memories of trauma from early in life can be repressed for a time, and then retrieved later, has been controversial. Anecdotally, it is common for survivors of childhood sexual abuse to repress these memories until adulthood, especially when abuse was prolonged and occurred at a very early age. When I have worked with clients who repressed their memories of abuse, they rarely feel as if they entirely forgot about the abuse. Rather, they explain that they always had fuzzy memories of abuse, but were confused about what happened. Many survivors did not consider the events abusive until they were older and could understand what sexual abuse is. Others always had a vague feeling that something bad must have happened, because they retained the emotional and bodily impressions of abuse. This makes sense in light of the nature of trauma memory, and how the explicit memory system is disrupted during sexual abuse but the implicit memory system records those impressions of terror and helplessness.

Most of the research about repressed and recovered memories focuses on explicit language-based memories. In other words, researchers try to see if survivors can tell them in words what happened to them, and then try to verify their stories. Researchers also try to see if they can fool the memory system by suggesting an event occurred that never actually happened, and then seeing if people 'remember' it.

It's true that people can be suggestible, and in laboratory settings memories can be malleable by presenting misleading information after an event has occurred.[v] However, all of these laboratory experiments aimed to insert a non-traumatic memory, like being lost in a shopping mall or losing a favorite toy. Because of the ethical issues involved, researchers cannot create a traumatic memory. The closest they have come is to try to create a memory of a painful and intrusive rectal exam, and none of the participants 'remembered' it.[vi] Since traumatic memories are fundamentally different than neutral memories, the research leads to the conclusion that it's very possible to misremember things from childhood, but *not* to misremember childhood sexual abuse.

In samples of women and men who experienced sexual abuse at a young age, repressing memories of the abuse is very common. One study found that almost 60% of survivors had at one time forgotten about the abuse.[vii] When women with a documented history of childhood sexual abuse (from hospital and human services records) were interview about their childhoods, 38% did not recall the abuse.[viii]

Dissociation may be another mechanism by which memories are repressed. At the moment of the trauma, dissociation occurs in order to protect the conscious psyche from being completely overwhelmed. Indeed, children are more vulnerable to trauma because they lack mature brain structures. The brain then pushes those memories deep into the subconscious. Later, the memories may resurface when we have a more mature brain, more psychological resources, and more social support. The mind senses that we have the capacity now, as adults, to face what happened.

If you suspect that you repressed memories of childhood sexual abuse, it's understandable to be worried about being believed. It's important to find a specialist that you feel comfortable talking to, and someone who makes you feel heard and validated. It's entirely appropriate when searching for a therapist to ask the therapist their thoughts and opinions about memory repression and childhood sexual abuse. Trust yourself. In order to do the hard work of recovering from childhood abuse you need support and understanding.

It's important to understand that memories do not necessarily need to be retrieved in order to heal. We may have a deep desire to understand exactly what happened in our childhood in order to explain how we feel today, or to shed light on troublesome behavioral or relationship patterns. Some paths of recovery do include re-visiting memories in order to process them. But for others, this is not helpful. If memories have been repressed for a long time, it may be very difficult or impossible to retrieve them. Furthermore, reaching far back into the past may be destabilizing in the present, which is counter-productive to healing.

Survivors Speak- Julia, Age 32

For some reason 21 was the age at which I began to understand in a more concrete way that I had been sexually abused and that my implicit memories of that trauma were not just delusions (as my family had suggested) or indicative of some in- born psychosis (as I had feared).

Having only implicit memories of the abuse that I endured, I was put in a rather confusing position. The validity of my trauma response (in the eyes of my family) seemed to hinge on whether or not I knew who my perpetrator was, how they abused me, and when the abuse occurred. But in hindsight, I don't doubt that (in the presence of explicit memories) some other reason would have been found to invalidate my beliefs about my abuse and my response to it.

The mental illnesses that plagued my family on every side were explained by my parents and my grandparents as an inherited defect that was to be hobbling but somehow endured with a smile. Both sets of my grandparents had been very zealous adherents to the tenants of their different Christian sects, Catholicism and Christian Science. From what I can tell from my parents' descriptions of their childhoods it seems that both sects had similar mental and physical health philosophies: if you're in pain it's because God is teaching you a lesson and if you pray and repent and you're still in pain, you must have done something monstrous. So I can see how in my family, it wouldn't be helpful to acknowledge abuse, and so much the better if we didn't tell ourselves that it was happening either. I went that extra mile to ensure that no one would ever, Ever, EVER know. As it turns out, my adorable-little-girl-of-a-self made the best available decision. So, I had (and to a frustrating extent I still have) amnesia.

Doesn't that sound like something that only exists in the context of daytime programming? Some woman on a Soap Opera gets hit hard on the head and she forgets who she is. Maybe other people know her story and maybe they don't. Maybe they lie to her and maybe they don't. Maybe she recovers and maybe she doesn't. But there is always a "before" and an "after." "Before you forgot who you were, you were this." "Before you forgot who you loved, you had loved these people in these ways." Often, there is an "after" that is a dramatic recovery. She doesn't recover from the same condition that her loved ones have suffered through. She didn't miss anyone or anything external, because she didn't even know to miss them. Her struggle was that she suffered from the kind of existential groundlessness that spans from "what soda do I drink?" to "why am I here in this café?" to "where do I find meaning? Any meaning?" The amnesiac is reunited with herself.

So I have (to varying degrees) been like that fictional Soap Star with one major exception, which is: for me, there is no "before I lost my memory" and no "after I recovered my memory." What progress I have made with piecing the specifics of my life together has been very slow and very painful and not one that I see as having an end. When I think of myself as a little kid and try to imagine my experience, I think that I was trying really hard not to experience much of what was happening to me, let alone remember it. When I watch horror movies I cover my eyes and plug my ears when it gets too scary and I'm certain that I have been covering my eyes and plugging my ears for a very long time.

Most of the progress that I have made has been in developing a greater understanding of the traumatic events that I do remember and working to find an identity that is not so reliant on explicit memories. This last one has probably been the hardest for me, but I've come a long way. I felt for most of my life that I didn't have much attachment to the world around me. I didn't have any long-term relationships with people or places or art or food or activities. I made arbitrary decisions about how to spend my time and where and with whom. I didn't have experience-based preferences for simple things like what I liked on my pizza.

Making it even more difficult to orient myself was that one of the symptoms of my PTSD is a foreshortened sense of the future. I was really just floating around in whatever void I inhabited between the past and the future. I have heard that space described as nirvana but I have also heard it described as purgatory. I believed that I was in hell. I wasn't raised with any religion, but up until four years ago, I believed I was in hell. I had believed that since I was a child.

I asked my mother for help when I was four or five years old. I told her that I wanted to die and she dismissed my statement as some sort of cognitive or linguistic glitch. At 21 I attempted to disclose some of my sexual abuse history to my mother and it went very poorly. It hadn't occurred to me that my mother had also been sexually abused but after hearing her response to my disclosure I'm certain that she was. I remembered being raped when I was a teenager and when I told her that she said that being raped was a normal part of being a woman and that I shouldn't make a big deal out of it. I then told her that I thought that I had been sexually abused as a child. Her response was that it was impossible and could never have happened because she had constantly watched me all the time throughout my childhood.

Nothing could have been further from the truth. My childhood memories are almost entirely memories of loneliness, spending days and days with babysitters and at the houses of family friends and relatives, wandering around my neighborhood alone, and the sort of domestic self-sufficiency that comes from not having someone to cook and clean for you. There is a good chance that my mother really doesn't remember it how I do. There is a good chance that my sister doesn't remember driving me to the houses of men who would pay to rape me. There's a very good chance that if I only know part of my story, I know almost nothing about theirs, and thankfully looks of confusion, hurt, and distrust at our family dinners are as bad as it gets for any of us now.

At 32 I still have fewer memories than most other people but I have a good understanding of how strong I am to have endured so much. I have been able to look closer at experiences that I had assumed where "okay" and understand them as painful and traumatic. I also have a future that is probably as long as anybody else's. I have found meaning and I have learned how to experience a range of emotions. I have learned how to love being loved by others.

I think that the most important lesson that I have learned from living with amnesia is that I have come very close to accepting the fluidity, complexity, and ultimate unknowability of any being, including myself. I can't open my mind up and take stock of my parts; I can only appreciate my fluid expressions of identity as they come. All I can do is forgive myself for my mistakes, give myself what I think I desire, and be very patient. And that's a pretty great way to live, regardless of how I got here.

Chapter 6: But it *Was* My Fault: Internalizing Blame as a Way to Gain Control

The path of healing begins with understanding. For survivors of sexual assault, simply understanding what happened to them and using the correct words is a momentous leap forward. Once this has happened, we move along our path. But no matter how far we move forward, or how much we understand about trauma effects and our traumatized brains, some things persist: self-blame, guilt, and shame.

Sexual assault breeds shame like nothing I have ever seen. Maybe it's because a sexual assault means someone has breached our most private barriers. Maybe it's due to the fact that sexual assault is still a taboo topic in our culture. Maybe it's because societal narratives hold out a vision of the individual in complete control of their lives. When misfortune comes, we automatically search for how that individual may have brought it upon themselves, even in the smallest of ways.

It's very common for survivors to feel on a very deep level that the sexual assault does define them. Survivors use words like dirty, broken, faulty, or disgusting to describe themselves. This sense of being somehow less than others is stubbornly persistent. Even when survivors intellectually understand the myth and facts about sexual assault, there is still a small voice that protests. It whispers, *you shouldn't have been drinking, you should have seen the red flags, you could have stopped it.* Even if our rational minds can rebut everything this shame-based voice says, somehow it doesn't ring true in our hearts and we continue to hold onto shame.

Why might this be? Like all trauma-related effects, the internalization of blame is a survival mechanism. It's scarier to believe that the world is an unsafe place than to believe we can't control what happens to us. When our psychological security is at stake, our minds accept the negative (self-blame) in order to hold onto the positive (the world is a safe place). If I believe that I could have stopped or avoided the sexual assault, then I can avoid that kind of attack in the future. This belief allows me to feel some control over my life, even though it carries self-blame. This feeling of control in the world is of paramount importance, and the price we pay is guilt.

This process of internalizing blame for sexual assault is especially pronounced for survivors of childhood sexual abuse. It's so critical for children to believe that the world is generally safe and that adults will care for them. Children are dependent on others, after all. Living in a completely unsafe world would cause a child to psychologically shut down and disintegrate to the point that it would damage their development. In order the avoid this, the child unconsciously justifies the abuse by concluding that if only they were good children, the abuse would stop. If you believe the abuse occurred because of something you are doing you can maintain hope for change. If only you can figure out the right things to do or to avoid doing, the abuse will stop. It is terrifying to face the reality that you are powerless in the face of adults who were untrustworthy, out of control, and abusive.

Furthermore, many children are told directly and repeatedly that they *are* to blame. This may happen during the abuse and when the survivor reaches out to others for help. This message then gets internalized. Some may replay those messages over and over in their minds as adults, without even recognizing the original source. For survivors with dissociative disorders, some parts of themselves may even take on the role of internal critic, repeating and reinforcing the messages of the abusers.

Judith Herman points out that "the sense of safety in the world, or basic trust, is acquired in earliest life in the relationship with [primary] caretakers. Originating with life itself, this sense of trust sustains a person throughout the lifecycle…the original experience of care makes it possible for human beings to envisage a world in which they belong, a world hospitable to human life."[i] Attachment to caregivers is of primary importance to create this basic trust in the world, and it must be salvaged, even in the face of abuse. Self-blame enables survivors to protect abusers, thus attempting to maintain some sort of attachment with important others. This may be especially the case when the abusers were family members or significant people who, at times, had something to offer in addition to abuse.

Children do not have a nuanced understanding of morality yet, and they can't comprehend that bad things happen to good people. They are left believing that bad things happen only to bad people, and that they are bad in some way because someone abused them.

Higher degrees of self-blame in survivors of childhood sexual assault are moderated by several factors. Research shows that self-blame is increased in survivors when the perpetrator was close to the child (like a relative or teacher), the abuse was repetitive and long lasting, and the child coped with the abuse at the time by repressing it or pretending that it didn't happen.[ii]

Blame to Shame: Shifting from Behavior to Character

For many survivors, this tendency to blame themselves for the assault begins with looking at their behaviors. For example, they may blame themselves for drinking too much alcohol around the time of the assault, hanging out with the wrong people, not overtly fighting their perpetrator, or not immediately reporting the abuse or assault.

This kind of blame centers on people's actions, and is the basis for guilt. Guilt is something we experience when we feel badly about our actions. Guilt about a sexual assault is bad enough, but all too often self-blame morphs into guilt's ugly cousin, shame. Shame is feeling badly about who we *are*, rather than what we *did*. Shame is feeling that we are, at a very deep level, not good enough. Shame is feeling that we do not belong in the world, and that if others really saw us and our fundamental flaws, that we would be rejected.

A leading researcher and writer on shame, Brene Brown, puts it this way:

> A clear way to see the difference is to think about this question: If you made a mistake that really hurt someone's feelings, would you be willing to say, "I'm sorry. I made a mistake"? If you're experiencing guilt, the answer is yes: "I MADE a mistake." Shame, on the other hand, is "I'm sorry. I AM a mistake." Shame doesn't just sound different than guilt; it feels different.[iii]

For survivors of sexual assault, shame can be deep and pernicious. Shame is what comes from describing the self as ugly, stupid, dirty, worthless, and disgusting. Shame is a very painful feeling; it's the experience of believing we are flawed and therefore are inherently unworthy of acceptance, belonging, and love. Shame makes us feel like we need to hide parts of ourselves in order to keep our relationships with others. Survivors have told me about the shame they feel around many things:

- Trauma symptoms
- Thoughts or fantasies about the perpetrator
- Facts of the abuse or assault
- Their ambivalent feelings about the perpetrator (usually the mix of hatred and affection)
- Their feelings towards themselves
- Behaviors that are meant to soothe in painful moments, but are embarrassing (examples include using drugs or alcohol, cutting, over-eating, impulse shopping, sexual behavior)
- Sexual fantasies that are deemed unacceptable (common ones include fantasies about being submissive)
- Their suspicion of others
- Violent fantasies involving attacking the perpetrator

Deep down, survivors often feel that parts of themselves are too strange or embarrassing or taboo to ever be brought to light. In this way, shame shows up in our relationships. We fear that others will abandon or reject us if they knew these embarrassing things. Further, we usually don't even want to acknowledge them to ourselves, and so our own relationship with our authentic self suffers.

One good self-test for shame is filling in the blanks in this sentence:

If people knew _____, they would surely _____.

Take a moment to write down your version of this sentence. You may have several different ones. Usually the first blank is filled in by something about ourselves that we don't like. The second blank most of the time reflects some kind of abandonment, ridicule, or shunning from others.

I asked some survivors to fill in these blanks:

If people knew that I still have a relationship with the man who sexually assaulted me, they would surely think I'm crazy.

If people know how much I drank that night, they would surely think I was 'crying rape.'

If people knew that I am scared to death of sex, they would surely never want to date me.

If people knew that I lied to protect my abuser, they would surely not trust my story.

Brene Brown, through her research on shame, discovered that shame is triggered by the appearance of *unwanted identities.* We all hold an idea of our ideal self. This is the self that we strive to be, and our ideal self is often influenced by our families, our friends, cultural messages, and our own values. An unwanted identity is a characteristic that flies in the face of our ideal self. An unwanted identity is usually one that is seen as negative, taboo, or unacceptable.

For survivors of sexual trauma, I have heard unwanted identities described as *broken, crazy, weak, irrational, used, pathetic, strange, tarnished, stained,* and *a victim.* I think the central theme among these words is the idea that the sexual assault makes someone damaged on a fundamental level, and that their psychological difficulties make them weak.

Of course no one wants to walk around in the world feeling like they are damaged and weak. All of our cultural messages praise strength and rationality. Normal trauma can look very abnormal from the outside. From the trauma seems to hijack our identity for a more unstable and vulnerable version of ourselves. Our ideal self seems very far away, like the perpetrator snatched it away from us. This makes us feel powerless all over again.

Moving through Shame toward Empathy

Shame is a normal human emotion and it's unavoidable in our culture of unattainable ideals. For survivors, shame is a valid and normal response to feeling powerless. In an effort to gain control over our lives and create the perception of a safe world, we find ourselves in self-blame and, eventually, in shame. Shame cannot be wished away or entirely avoided, but we can work with shame by recognizing it and diffusing it through empathy and connection.

The first step to moving constructively through shame is recognizing our shame and the triggers that send us into that shame. This includes becoming aware of what shame feels like, both physically and emotionally. Survivors have told me that shame feels like:

- My stomach dropping five feet.
- Feeling very hot all over my body.
- Finding it difficult to breathe.

- Feeling entirely alone, and thinking that I deserve it.
- A metallic taste in my mouth.
- A sudden nauseous feeling in my belly, and my throat tightening.
- Feeling intensely uncovered, like everyone can see all of my secrets.
- A strong urge to run and hide from everyone.
- Wanting to punish myself, since I feel like a bad person.

Shame triggers are very individual. Survivors of sexual assault experience shame around a wide variety of triggers. To identify triggers, Brown asks us to answer the following questions about our wanted and unwanted identities.

I want to be perceived as

_____.

I do *not* want to be perceived as

_____.

Shame can be triggered whenever we find that we are falling into those unwanted identities. Being aware of our triggers empowers us, because in moments of shame we can deploy our best weapons: empathy and connection.

Empathy is the capacity to recognize the emotions of others. It's that ability you have to see things from another's perspective. Once you put yourself in another's place, you can understand why they feel the way they do. Even if you don't agree with their emotional response, you can step inside their experience for a moment and see that their response is valid from their perspective. Our thoughts and feelings always make sense within the framework of our experience and worldview.

When moving through shame and coping with a sexual assault, we need to tap into empathy *for ourselves*. Your self in trauma is different from your everyday self, but it is a valid expression of your feelings and attempts to cope. It's easy want to disown our "trauma self" and look at that self as crazy, irrational, damaged, or a victim. We want to create distance between our "trauma self" and our true self because we do not want those identities. This disconnection, however, leads to shame.

Practice empathy for yourself, specifically the self that is dealing with trauma and all of its uncomfortable effects. It's important to see your own emotional experience from the perspective of a traumatized individual. This individual is coping with daily life the best that they can. Their trauma effects are valid, normal, and understandable. Those strange thoughts and "irrational" emotions are a by-product of a body and brain in healing; it's an organism desperately seeking safety in an unsafe world. Have compassion and empathy for that person who is struggling so much and doing the best they can in the moment.

Recognize that you are not broken or damaged; you are healing. Just as your arm looks and feels different when it's healing from a fracture, your self is in healing right now and is in a transitory state. Practicing empathy and compassion for ourselves allows us room to own all of those thoughts and emotions that we try to divorce ourselves from. An internal dialogue for practicing empathy may sound something like this:

I'm having those thoughts about the perpetrator again. I hate him so much, I want to kill him. I don't think I'm a violent person, though. I'm aware of some shame around these recurring thoughts, and it makes me worry about the type of person I am. But I can see how these fantasies are a way for me to access anger and to feel control, and that seems normal given what I've gone through. I remember reading that those types of thoughts are really normal. I must be hurting a lot, and I deserve some gentleness. I know that I won't feel like this forever, and the healing process is uncomfortable. I'll try to cut myself some slack around this.

Or this:

Tom didn't call me back after that first date. He must somehow know that I'm damaged and broken inside, that something's not right. This always happens, and I hate it. He's right to run away from this craziness. I'm aware of shame that comes up around rejection like this. I need to remember that this sense of being stained is a result of self-blame that I've definitely internalized. This is a normal and valid thing to happen in the wake of trauma, even if it's really uncomfortable. It's so painful to feel this way, and I would extend kindness to anyone in that kind of self-loathing, so I'll try to do that for myself. It might be a hard day today, moving through this shame and these feelings of rejection. I'm going to remind myself to go easy, and do something that makes me feel like myself, and maybe talk to some friends about it.

Notice that in this thought pattern there is self-validation, compassion, and engaging of our logical brain. In moments of emotional pain, we need to connect to our experience through awareness and bring empathy into the picture. It's also very helpful to remind ourselves of what we know about normal trauma effects, and see the internal trauma-based logic of our reactions.

It's hard to acknowledge shame, but awareness is the first step to moving through it. Become aware of any shame you are carrying with regards to the assault itself, or its effects. Be kind to and compassionate with yourself. As difficult as shame is to work with, it does dissipate over time when named and met with knowledge and empathy.

Survivors Speak: Nicole, Age 45

My journey through shame has been long and difficult. I can say now that it got better for me once I started to face it. My history of abuse was pushed away for so long because I feared that it would be more than I could bear. But as the years went on, I found there to be more suffering attached to putting it off, to disowning my own experience. I felt so ashamed of what happened to me, and I also felt shame around how I dealt with it for so long.

I had a one-two punch. First, I was abused as a child by someone I knew and trusted. I felt bad and disgusting, like I was sub-human and carried a darkness within me that I had to hide from everyone else. On top of that, I felt like I was a very weak person for having so many psychological problems. I dealt with them by using alcohol and drugs, and basically shutting everyone good out of my life. The shame just hangs over everything in your life; it colors it and dulls it like a sepia-toned picture. I could never experience anything fully with that shame in the way.

I tried to punish myself in various ways. I didn't take good care of my body or my health. When I was younger and couldn't stand my emotions, I would punch the wall or bang my head against something. I would sabotage my chances at good jobs and healthy relationships.

All I can say is that it gets better as you face it. It hurts, more than anything I've ever known, because now I have to feel the feelings I had as a child along with the maturity of an adult to know exactly what those feelings are about...but I know I'm healing. I can feel it, and my family and support group tell me they can see it.

Not being ashamed of myself may take a while...so much of her verbal abuse was about how shameful and filthy and dirty I was. Sometimes I feel like the stereotypical "rape victim" in a Lifetime movie, huddled in the shower trying to scrub off the dirt.

I know now that I am not to blame. The disgust belongs to my abuser, not to me. I need to have compassion for myself; that really helps. It helps to remember that I really didn't do anything wrong, and all those ways of coping that I'm ashamed of, those were the best I could manage at the time. I still fall back into those old habits, but I'm slowly moving away from them. I'm starting to believe that peace might just be possible for me.

It hurts to deal with all of this , but the fear I built up around facing it was worse than the actual pain of facing it—I already lived through the worst of it once, and I owe it to the child I once was, who had no hope or help, to honor her by remembering and grieving.

Chapter 7: I Can't Believe This Happened Again: The Re-Victimization Cycle

It's very common for survivors of sexual assault to experience more trauma or victimization later in their lives. It's often confusing, and may lead to shame and self-blame. This is often a sensitive and difficult topic, but it's very important to validate and normalize this experience. Like anything that brings shame, it's important to speak it. In this chapter, we will explore the process of re-victimization and explore some possible causes.

It's a well-known fact that survivors of sexual abuse and sexual assault are more likely to experience additional trauma in their lifetimes. This is especially true for survivors of childhood sexual assault. It's important to make a distinction here. It is not true that there is a "type" of person who is victimized, but it *is* true that earlier trauma experiences make survivors more vulnerable to later sexual assault, domestic violence, or simply being taken advantage of by others. These vulnerabilities can be thought of as wounds that we carry, and these wounds make survivors more susceptible to future victimization. Of course abuse and assault are never the victim's fault, but exploring the ways we might be vulnerable to mistreatment leads to greater understanding, self-validation, and empowerment.

We know that the risk of repeated victimization is about doubled for survivors of childhood sexual abuse.[i] Furthermore, one study found that for survivors of childhood incest (i.e. sexual abuse by a family member), the risk increases to two-thirds.[ii] It's a well-documented connection in the scientific literature. At present, there are many different theories about why this happens, and I will include some in this chapter.

Survivors often feel as if they are marked in some way. One of my clients explained that she feels like she has "a sign on my forehead that says 'abuse me, I'm an easy target.'" They may feel like they are destined to experience maltreatment. When victimization happens over and over, it's easy to understand this feeling. When this pattern of re-victimization presents itself, it's understandable to conclude that it's somehow deserved. You might think, "If this happens again and again, maybe I'm asking for it, or there really is something wrong with me."

It's incorrect to think that survivors are somehow consciously seeking out more trauma. It is true, however, that survivors may find themselves in dangerous situations or abusive relationships more often than people who were never sexually assaulted. Why might this be?

The Devil You Know

There's a saying that I use when talking about re-victimization: *Better the devil you know than the devil you don't.* This basically means that it's usually better to deal with someone or something you are familiar with, even if they are far from ideal, than to take a risk with an unknown person or thing.

For someone who has had to survive sexual abuse, trauma has become their norm. Normalizing their experience is a survival mechanism, a way to cope with the trauma when it was happening and still function in their lives. If abuse occurs at an early age, especially within the family, the child has no outside perspective on their experience. When we are children, all that we experience we think is 'normal' because we've never had a contradictory experience. We learn what to expect from the world (i.e. what's 'normal') within our families and social networks. If those social networks include abuse, we conclude that this is the way of things, and we learn to expect and come to terms with abuse.

Survivors become good at living with abuse. Their inner genius and wisdom allows them to thrive in the midst of it. They learn to cope with the devil they know. The downside, of course, is that the devil they *don't* know becomes a scary and threatening thing. From the outside, a life without abuse or trauma, a life filled with appropriate boundaries and loving relationships, looks like heaven. Through the lens of trauma, however, this life can look intimidating and unreachable. Survivors often tell me that they feel they have "missed the memo" about relationships—that they just don't know the rules of engagement for healthy relationships, and so they inevitably end up in relationships that span from co-dependent to outright abusive.

The Comfort of Predictability

Humans are, at the core, creatures of habit. Even the most spontaneous amongst us feels stress when placed in a position without any predictability. Anyone who has traveled abroad can attest to this. What we call 'Culture Shock' is simply how we feel when we can't predict how others will act. We are always engaged in a subtle, culturally prescribed social dance with the people around us. Generally, we know how to act around others and how to get what we need from them.

Sadly, abuse and boundary violations can become predictable for trauma survivors. There is a certain comfort in predictability, and survivors can unconsciously cling to the repetitive pattern that they know and have learned to master. Re-victimization, while never enjoyed or consciously sought out by the survivor, can have a certain comfort in its familiarity.

One survivor, a 32 year-old woman who was abused
as a child by her uncle, puts it this way:

*It's very weird to say, but I feel like I can handle abusers, and
so the abusive men I always end up with don't trigger any red
flags for me. Some of them have raped me. Others have just
been very jealous or controlling. When a nice guy comes
along, I can feel panic building. It's like he's an alien creature
that I don't know what to do with. I think that, unconsciously,
a nice guy who treats me with respect is more threatening than
the one who should send up red flags. It feels really
backwards, and it's so frustrating because I know this is due to
my childhood. It feels like I'm stuck in this cycle because I'm
afraid to do anything differently. More than that, I feel like I
don't know how."*

When survivors describe this common (and very
understandable) pattern in their relationships, I reflect back to
them that this pattern *has* been working in some way. Even if
the only way it's working is providing some kind of stability,
that's still functional. We always do what works, even if it's
not perfect or doesn't make sense to others around us. Being in
a predictable situation, even if it's not ideal or what we
consciously want for ourselves, can keep survivors stuck in

unhealthy relationships.

Blind Spots

Everyone has their blind spots. A blind spot can be thought of as a signal, warning, or trigger that we fail to see or notice. Another phrase for a blind spot in psychology terms is *cognitive bias*. Our cognitive biases are the subtle ways that we distort our reality. In other words, we don't perceive our reality as objective; we all have our blind spots and biases that make our worldview unique.

Usually we are completely unaware of our blind spots, but we can become more conscious of them through introspection, getting good feedback from others, and from working with a therapist. With sexual assault survivors, that there are some common blind spots that contribute to re-victimization.

One is a blind spot around how we gauge others' actions towards us. When someone oversteps our boundaries, or is too intrusive, demanding, or controlling, we usually can recognize this for what it is and put a stop to it. Survivors have difficulty with this. Since their boundaries were violated in such an extreme way, lesser boundary violations often don't register. This makes survivors relatively easy to manipulate or take advantage of. This pattern can happen in all kinds of relationships, and can be relatively mild or more severe. One survivor, a 45 year-old woman who was raped when she was in college, talks about this pattern at work:

I constantly feel like I'm a victim at work. My boss—it seems like she's being nice and asking me to do things, and before I know it I've agreed to take care of her dry cleaning and get her coffee. It's like I don't notice the little things until I feel really overwhelmed and get really angry. None of these errands are really my job to do. I've been told in the past that I can be like a doormat, but I just don't notice it happening until it becomes more extreme.

Or this example from a 30 year-old survivor sharing about her relationship patterns:

Ever since I was raped in my teens, I've tended to seek out these really masculine, strong guys. I guess they make me feel safe, but I also seem to attract really controlling, jealous guys. After the guy that raped me, I guess I didn't realize that those behaviors were abusive too. It seemed reasonable to me, and kind of safe. It sounds really bad, I know, but I just couldn't see what everyone else saw about these guys. That they were controlling jerks.

In general, survivors of sexual trauma have difficulty spotting danger or over-reaching in their relationships. This leads to a cycle of re-victimization and difficulty in setting healthy boundaries. Judith Herman, in her book *Trauma and Recovery*, puts it this way:

> For too long psychiatric opinion has simply reflected the crude social judgment that survivors "ask for" abuse...More commonly, repeated abuse is not actively sought for but rather is passively experienced as a dreaded but unavoidable fate and is accepted as the inevitable price of relationships. Many survivors have such profound deficiencies in self-protection that they can barely imagine themselves in a position of agency or choice. The idea of saying no to the emotional demands of a parents, spouse, lover or authority figure may be practically inconceivable. Thus, it is not uncommon to find survivors who...permit major intrusions without boundaries or limits.[iii]

One proposed mechanism for these blind spots is the dissociative coping style that many survivors employ.

Learning early in life to block out trauma can lend itself to creating more blind spots than people who never had to use dissociation to get along in life. Although the tendency to dissociate or detach in one's life can lead to these types of blind spots, this process can be reversed by becoming more aware of boundaries in relationships and working to re-establish healthy relationships. Working on boundaries is often a big piece of the healing process.

Low Self-Esteem and Re-victimization

We all have days or phases in our lives when we just don't like ourselves. We may dislike our physical appearance, our personality, or our behaviors. It's normal to go through a process of being self-critical, and if we hold compassion for ourselves along with our criticism, we can use those observations to grow and move toward a more ideal self. Survivors of sexual assault, however, tend to have low self-esteem, and this low opinion of themselves is not a phase; it's more pervasive and insidious, and has real-world consequences.

Self-esteem is both a judgment about the self and a general attitude towards the self. Self-esteem encompasses both our emotions about ourselves (positive or negative) and beliefs about our worthiness for respect, acceptance, and love from others. Research shows that survivors of sexual assault have significantly lower self-esteem than non-survivors, and that this low self-esteem tends to be stable over time.[iv] Even the *thought* of rape can lead to lower self-esteem and more negative self-evaluations. Using women that had never been raped in an experiment, researchers demonstrated that just being asked to think about rape led to negative answers on a self-esteem survey.[v]

The emotions and beliefs we have about ourselves influence our behaviors, especially in situations where someone is taking advantage of us or crossing boundaries. If, deep down, we don't have a high opinion of ourselves, we are not surprised or angry when someone doesn't treat us well. Like we discussed earlier in the chapter about shame, the internalized "dirtiness" that sexual assault survivors carry with them implies a belief that they are really not worthy of respect, care, or love. If we are treated like objects to be used for others' gratification, then we learn that we are only good for satisfying other people's desires rather than our own.

Survivors learn through experience that others matter more than they do, and so they act accordingly. It's understandable, although tragic, to see this point of view. Survivors live in a world that promotes sexual objectification and violence. Our culture blames victims. Sexual trauma is misunderstood and survivors are invalidated at every turn.

Victim blaming is unfortunately the norm. Most importantly, in each survivor's experience of sexual assault they learn that the perpetrator's desires mattered more than their safety. We take cues about our own self-worth from the world around us.

Low self-esteem plays a big role in re-victimization. If we feel generally negative about ourselves and don't believe we deserve respect, it's easy to fall into dysfunctional relationships with others or engage in risky behavior.

In my work with survivors, I've seen self-esteem slowly shift over time as survivors learn about their own strengths and resiliency. As self-esteem increases, survivors feel more empowered to hold healthy boundaries with others, and seek out relationships with supportive and respectful people.

Re-writing the End of the Story

Re-victimization, in certain circumstances, can be thought of as a form of *reenactment.* Reenactment is a psychological term referring to the tendency of individuals to re-create old relationship patterns. All people do this to different degrees, not only survivors of sexual abuse. Usually these repetitions mirror our early experiences, and our family experiences are particularly salient. For example, a man who grew up in a chaotic household due to an alcoholic father may find himself unwittingly creating chaos in his own life. Or a woman whose father was unavailable and emotionally cold may find herself again and again in relationships with men who are also unavailable and unable to connect with her emotionally.

Reenactment is one of the oldest ideas in psychology, and is a well-known pattern. Sigmund Freud, the father of modern psychology, referred to these patterns as "the need to restore an earlier state of things."[vi] This need arises from a deep-seated and often unconscious desire to work through the earlier experience, and particularly to take an active versus passive role in the relational dynamics.

In a sense, trauma survivors are trying to set the stage again and work toward a different ending to the story. They seek out ways they can contradict their original experience. They want to prove to themselves that it can be different, that they can have mastery over their lives and control the ways in which they are sexual.

A survivor I worked with for almost 2 years struggled mightily with re-victimization:

When I was raped last year, I was so completely shocked by the experience. I was out on a first date, and this man just forced himself on me. After it happened, I think I was in denial, but at the same time I knew that he raped me. It was so confusing because he acted like it didn't happen when he dropped me off at home. Then I did something that I'm so ashamed of, and which confused me for such a long time. A few days after the rape, I called him and asked to meet again. Then I had sex with him. It was like I was on a mission to sleep with him. I wasn't attracted to him, but something deep inside me needed to prove to myself that I could choose who to have sex with and when. Maybe I was trying to dominate him. Or violate him. I don't really know. I was so embarrassed and I thought I was crazy for doing that. I also thought that, since I chose to have sex with the perpetrator, that the previous rape didn't really count. I've learned now that this isn't the case, and the rape wasn't my fault. I also understand that I was trying to take back my control and my power. It was a strange way to do it, but trauma is a strange thing.

Here's another example from a survivor in her late twenties:

I knew I was abused as a kid, but I didn't start to think about it much until I was in my twenties. I sort of became obsessed with it, and I couldn't wrap my mind around it or let it go. During that phase of my life, I found myself doing things that were really out of character for me. I would go to bars all the time, alone, and drink way too much. I never did that before, and I knew it wasn't a really safe thing to do. Also during this time, I was sexually assaulted twice by men that I met when I was out drinking. I think it sounds crazy, but I believe that I was sort of daring the world. I think on a deep level I wanted someone to try to assault me again, so that I could stop it. I have fantasies of beating guys up, and I wanted to do it and prove to myself that I was strong. Of course, it didn't end up that way and it was a tough time in my life. I had a lot of shame around it. I felt that I branded as a life-long victim because it kept happening.

Ultimately, these attempts at control and mastery usually don't work in the way that survivors wish. Often, reenactment leads to re-victimization and further trauma, rather than empowerment and resolution. In order the break this cycle it's important to understand how reenactment works and accept that it's normal. Once we can see these patterns we can seek mastery in healthy ways.

The Helper Inside

One of the more positive effects of trauma is that our own suffering can lead to increased awareness of the suffering of others. We become more compassionate and empathetic because we know what it feels like. Survivors of sexual trauma are some of the most sensitive and compassionate people that

I've ever met. Sometimes they take on the role of caretaker in their relationships and even in their careers.

Although caring for others can be rewarding and help create meaning from our own trauma, this compassionate nature can also make us vulnerable to potential perpetrators or dependent people. People looking for victims can pick up on this tendency for caretaking and use survivors for their own purposes.

Even in situations where there is no outright abuse or manipulation, survivors can fall into a pattern of continuously taking on the responsibilities of others. Caretaking can be very exhausting, and often the caretaker neglects their own needs in the process. Too much caretaking can point to problems in our boundaries, or the deep need to take away the pain of others. Playing the part of a people-pleaser can lead survivors to feel like they are being victimized all over again. They feel intruded upon, and that their boundaries are being violated. Even well-meaning friends and family members can trip these wires for survivors because there is a pre-existing sensitivity for acutely feeling any boundary violation.

It's important for survivors of sexual violence to cultivate their compassion mindfully, being sure to balance empathy with independence. Be careful to not take on other people's responsibilities or put others' needs before your own.

Combating Shame about Re-victimization

Re-victimization is a difficult topic. It often brings up feelings of shame and embarrassment. It's difficult to balance the reality of abuse with the recognition of behavior patterns that may contribute to repeated trauma. I want to reiterate here that sexual assault, abuse, or manipulation is never the victim's fault. Re-victimization is a reality for many survivors, but it does not point to any inherent weakness or a desire to be abused. When we look at the cycle of re-victimization from a trauma lens, its logic and normality will appear.

If the themes in this chapter resonate with you, my hope is that you can arrive at a place of compassion. Recognize that re-victimization is normal and an understandable response to trauma. Just like with the trauma effects we learned about, be mindful that efforts toward wholeness can sometimes result in discomfort and suffering. Re-victimization is about the normalization of trauma, seeking mastery and control, and internalizing messages from the outside world.

Survivors Speak-Jane, Age 31

My first love turned into my first hate. A boy I went to high school with was my first boyfriend, and we were definitely in puppy-love. At first it was great, and I was so excited to have a real boyfriend like my friends did. It quickly spiraled into an abusive relationship. He started to get really angry with me, and would punch walls and tell me I was lucky it wasn't my face he was hitting. He never physically abused me, but he used the threat of violence to get what he wanted. It was really scary at first but I think eventually I just became numb.

He also raped me three times. The first time, I remember being so scared and shocked that I just froze. Afterward, I told him that I wanted to slow our relationship down and did not want to have sex again until I was ready. He said he was okay with that, but two more times he forced me to have sex with him. By the third time, he simply held me down and did it. I was lying on my stomach, crying, and he was biting at my back and neck and telling me to be quiet.

That was the last straw, and although he frightened me I broke up with him. I told some of my friends that he was being jealous and angry, and they stood by me. I never told them about the rapes. This was close to graduation, so I simply avoided him at school and then went off to college and tried to forget about it.

I didn't really date much in college, but after college I felt like I wanted a relationship. I noticed that when I started dating I found myself in relationships with guys that were really jealous or explosive, or even outright abusive. One guy forced himself on me, and I even continued to date him for a few months afterward. I felt like I was flawed in some way, like I had a sign on my back that said 'go ahead and abuse me, I'll take it.' After every abusive incident, I would feel so hopeless. I knew that I wasn't consciously trying to be abused but I always ended up in the same place.

I decided to take a step back from dating and work on myself. I did a lot of reading and talked to a therapist. I slowly learned to see how I was contributing to my situation, while at the same time acknowledging that I was not to blame for any abuse or maltreatment from men. It was hard for me to tease the two apart, but once I could really see what was happening I could grieve for the original abuse. I realized that since my first experience with sex was abusive, I became accustomed to it.

I came to see that I sought out men to date that I saw more as projects than boyfriends. I thought I could 'fix' these guys that were rough around the edges. Their jealousy and controlling nature made me feel safe. I hated that I felt this way, but once I let it come to the surface I could begin to make different choices. I had to learn how to be vulnerable, and to stop trying to fix other people.

I am just beginning to date again, and it's been a hard process. I have a lot of support from close friends, family, and my therapist. I know that I'm not broken or flawed, but I do have to navigate the dating world a bit more carefully.

Chapter 8: Toward Recovery

Healing is a process, and the journey is a difficult one. Survivors of sexual trauma have used the wisdom of their bodies and minds to adapt and function in spite of trauma. Moving toward recovery means sloughing off those old ways of coping and learning new ones. The healing process involves having a direct relationship to our pasts, and touching our pain rather than avoiding it. One survivor put it this way:

"I had to learn how to live in the midst of this trauma, because I couldn't make it go away. Some of it I was able to ignore and deny. Some of it I combated with over-compensating. Other times I medicated myself as best I could with alcohol and shopping. It was like I had built this nest for myself to insulate me from the pain of it all. And it did work, in a way and for a time. Then my nest got a bit stale and smelly, and it was causing problems of its own. I got too big for the nest, and I needed to fly out of it. That was really scary at first, but it was worth it."

Stages of Recovery

Most researchers and practitioners in the field of trauma treatment think about recovery as happening in stages. Dr. Judith Herman[i] proposes three stages: Safety,

Remembrance and Mourning, and Reconnection. It's important to remember that recovery is an inherently complex process and does not follow a predictable linear pattern. You may feel you are in one stage one day and another stage on a different day. You may feel like you are solidly in stage three, and then all of the sudden be thrown back to stage one. Use these stages as a model, but not necessarily as a measure of your own progress. Herman used the analogy of a spiral for the recovery process, where "earlier issues are continually revisited on a higher level of integration."[ii]

Stage One: Safety

Recovery begins by establishing safety. Not only is physical safety extremely important, but so is emotional and mental safety. Survivors may feel unsafe in the world because of their hyperarousal. Additionally, survivors feel unsafe in their very beings. Their emotions and thoughts feel out of control. Intrusive thoughts, flashbacks, and nightmares are not under our complete control. Recall our discussion of brain dysregulation in Chapter 4; establishing safety means attaining some measure of regulation in the brain and body.

It's important in this stage to attend to basic needs by focusing on The Big Three (sleep, exercise, and diet). It can also be helpful to practice relaxation to help re-establish a calm baseline. Safety also means learning about and practicing some tools to re-regulate yourself after a trigger or during a particularly difficult moment. In Chapter 10 we will explore more tools for coping that are helpful in this stage.

Establish a safe environment for yourself at the beginning of your recovery process. Everyone needs a safe space, a refuge from stress and a place to simply be. Usually this space is your home, but changes may need to happen in order to make your home the refuge that you deserve. Some survivors have redecorated or moved their furniture around. Others have brought soothing objects into their home, like favorite candles or favorite foods. Some survivors want quiet, while others make sure to have their favorite music on hand or fill their home with supportive people. Survivors who live with family or roommates may establish boundaries or structure to make their environments calm.

Another important part of establishing safety is creating a good support system. Your support system includes all the people in your life who are willing and able to help you in your recovery. Not all (or even any) of these people need to know that you were sexually assaulted or the details of the assault itself. If it does not feel good to share this, you can simply state that you are going through a hard time, and you may call on them for support. Support can be many different things. It may mean talking about how you feel, or about your day. It could mean simply having company around the house when you don't want to be alone. Your support people can do activities with you, or simply help you get out of the house. You may want a daily or weekly check-in from a friend or family member. It's important for you to be in control and to ask for what you need.

In the early days of this journey, it can be tempting to isolate yourself. Sexual trauma is an isolating issue, and you may struggle with feelings of embarrassment or shame. It's very important to reach out to others as much as you feel comfortable so that you have a support system in place. At this stage, a support system might include a therapist or a support group. In the next chapter I will discuss the option of therapy in more detail.

Don't rush through this very important stage. Doing the work of recovering from trauma is inherently destabilizing and difficult, and it's important to have a strong foundation of safety for the journey.

Stage Two: Remembrance and Mourning

Once safety is established, the next task in healing is both remembering the trauma (to the best of your ability, keeping in mind that specific memories of abuse are not necessary) and processing all of the feelings that accompany it. These may include sadness, anger, frustration, disappointment, betrayal, and grief. Remember that the intrusive trauma effects are a guidepost here; although uncomfortable, these intrusive thoughts and persistent memories deserve our attention, our compassion, and our witness.

Most people think about this stage as a form of *catharsis*. Catharsis means a purification or "purge" of intense emotions. When I start trauma therapy with clients, many times they expect to have a few intense meetings where they recount their trauma, cry a lot, and then feel better on the other side. For better or worse, this part of the healing journey is not a one-time event. We may need to revisit certain memories more than once, or experience uncomfortable emotions many times over. Just like grieving the loss of a loved one, mourning does not mean having one "good cry" and then never feeling sad again. It's a process of witnessing and honoring our trauma experience in a safe environment, and re-working our narrative so that it reflects reality, acknowledges our suffering, and celebrates our strengths. Judith Herman writes about mourning in this way:

> The descent into mourning is at once the most
> necessary and the most dreaded task of this
> stage of recovery. Patients often fear the task
> is insurmountable, that once they allow
> themselves to start grieving, they will never

stop…She may consciously refuse to grieve as a way of denying victory to the perpetrator. In this case it is important to reframe [mourning] as an act of courage rather than humiliation. To the extent the patient is unable to grieve she is cut off from herself and robbed of an important part of her healing. Reclaiming the ability to feel the full range of emotions, including grief, must be understood as an act of resistance rather than submission to the perpetrator's intent. Only through mourning everything that she has lost can the patient discover her indestructible inner life.[iii]

Being sexually assaulted does change you. It's impossible to have such a traumatic experience and not be altered. We need to mourn what we have lost because of the assault. It may be our innocence or a sense of trust in others. It may be that we grieve over our former self. There is always loss when sexual violence is experienced.

Not only do survivors need to honor their pain by grieving what was lost, but they have the added burden of grieving things that they will never have due to the abuse they suffered. Especially for survivors of childhood sexual assault, there is the loss of an irreplaceable abuse-free childhood. They mourn the basic trust in the world that they will simply never have in the way someone with a safe childhood possesses. For survivors of sexual assault as adults, there is the loss of a life lived without the specter of abuse. A survivor once said to me, "You can't un-know what you already know." The sheer finality of sexual violence also deserves our attention and mourning.

It's in this stage that most survivors struggle with anger. A very justifiable anger is the result of the deep understanding of what we have lost at the hands of the perpetrator. Anger is pointing us toward our inherent goodness, and signaling that we truly did not deserve the abuse we experienced. In this way, anger can be healing.

It's also difficult to experience anger, especially for women who are socialized to believe that they should not be angry but always warm, forgiving, and cooperative. It's tempting to try to 'do something' with our anger. Experiencing intense anger can feel very helpless if we can't lash out. I see this sense of helplessness manifest most often in revenge fantasies revolving around the perpetrator. It could be imagining hurting him or her or making their actions known publicly to try to humiliate them. It can take the form of a mirror image of the trauma itself, with the roles of perpetrator and victim reversed.

I always try to normalize revenge fantasies of survivors. Often they feel embarrassed about them, or worried that their thoughts mean they will actually act on them. In the vast majority of cases, these thoughts are just thoughts, and they are healthy to the extent that they reinforce the fact that the perpetrator alone is responsible for the assault, and therefore is an appropriate target for angry feelings.

Delving into our memories and uncomfortable emotions is a daunting task, but it is a necessary step to healing. One of my favorite quotes that I use to explain the healing process is from a Robert Frost poem: "The best way out is always through."[iv] I remind survivors that our memories and emotions are crying out for our attention because they need to be processed in order to move forward. Continually avoiding them is tempting and comfortable, but is a temporary solution. Having a very direct and mature relationship with our reality is difficult, but is also healing.

Stage Three: Reconnection

Judith Herman calls the third and final stage of healing 'reconnection' to emphasize the importance of re-establishing our connections to ourselves and others in order to truly move on from trauma. After facing the past with courage and compassion, we turn toward the future. After mourning what was lost, we look to creating a new self, a self that integrates all of our experiences, both good and bad. This stage of healing is about reclaiming our power, our agency, and our world with the knowledge of our intrinsic strength.

Herman points out that "helplessness and isolation are the core experiences of psychological trauma," while "empowerment and reconnection are the core experiences of recovery."[v] Reconnection with the self really begins in stage one, where the survivor begins to listen to his or her needs and gauges reactions to the environment. It continues in stage two with the experiencing of difficult emotions and the interaction with individual memories. In stage three, reconnection with the self involves acknowledging a new story about the self, one that adds the role of 'survivor' to our other roles and identities. Identities such as daughter, son, friend, co-worker, musician, hard worker, etc., expand to include 'survivor of sexual violence.' Our survivor identity is no longer our *only* identity. It's certainly important, but does not in itself define who we are.

Reconnection with others involves learning to trust and take risks in relationships again. Being willing to be vulnerable and let others in is a sign of reconnection. This stage also includes rediscovering the ability to be sexual with a partner or alone. The sexual connection may be different than it was before the assault, but it is both safe and pleasurable. In all social situations, it's normal to feel awkward in this stage as you try to reconnect with others. One client of mine said she felt like she was experiencing "adolescence all over again…it's like I don't know how to act around people, especially men I am interested in dating."

This stage is usually where survivors begin to reconnect to society as a whole. You may be much more aware of sexual assault as a social issue, or more sensitive to subtle victim-blaming cues that are rife in public dialogue. Some survivors choose to connect with others who have been assaulted through groups or advocacy organizations. The majority of cities and towns have a rape crisis center or other non-profit organization whose mission involves combating sexual assault. See the Resources section at the end of the book for more information.

Taking Control

A central aspect of sexual trauma is helplessness. In addition, many of the effects of trauma are out of our direct control. As a result, it's important, in the healing process, for the survivor to have as much control as possible. You are in control of your process; listen to your own internal cues to help guide you. Even when there is shared control, such as when a survivor partners with a therapist, the survivor should be in control of the pace of therapy and be empowered to share what's working and what's not working in the therapy sessions.

As you enter your healing process it's crucial to step into the role of the competent director of your life. Even when working with therapists and doctors, you are always the expert on you. I believe that everyone, in their own way, strives towards health and wholeness. Even in the midst of trauma, survivors cope the best way that they can. Deep down, you know what you need and how to orient toward the kind of support that works best for you.

Being a competent director for you requires awareness and an attitude of openness to learning new things. Survivors often feel that they have not been themselves since the sexual assault. This is a valid and understandable effect of trauma as we struggle to understand our identity as a survivor. Similarly, the "you" in recovery from trauma will be different than the "you" that is not in a healing process. It's important to monitor how you feel physically and emotionally to discover what works for you, even if what you discover is new.

One survivor, a 30 year-old man who was molested by his uncle, describes the process this way:

I never thought I was a touchy-feely person. I knew I needed to do something to help me get over my past, and I was resigned to doing some therapy. I was willing to talk to someone for a while, but it took some time for me to realize that it was a much more active process than I had anticipated. I thought I would come, a therapist would ask me questions, I would answer them and then feel better. I found that the process didn't work until I really took control. I found that a support group was integral to my process. I had to be more open than I was before. I wanted my therapist to find a group for me, and push me in there so that I wouldn't have to go out of my comfort zone. But my therapist made me find that group myself, and make the calls and show up. Throughout my healing process I tried some new things that did help, and I was able to let go of what didn't. I took up boxing, because that seemed to help me work through my anger. It's a funny combination; on the one hand, I needed to hit some things, and on the other I needed to open up and cry.

Expanding Your World

Sexual trauma and its effects shrink our world. With triggers scattered around us like land mines, we do the best we can to walk around them, using avoidance to cope. This strategy has its time and place, and it helps us to survive both the trauma itself and its immediate aftermath. We can't really begin our healing (which means, for one, interrupting those avoidance patterns) until we establish safety and support. Once we begin our healing and deliberately step into those mental and emotional spaces that we have been avoiding, our world begins to expand. Places we previously feared to tread once again become part of our territory.

One metaphor I like to use when explaining trauma is that of horse blinders. Blinders are metal devices put onto a horse's face that block its peripheral vision. In effect, the horse has tunnel vision and can only see directly in front of it. This helps the horse to not become startled by its environment. In early healing from trauma, survivors can feel as if they have "trauma blinders" on their faces; they can only see, hear, and focus on the trauma itself. It feels all-consuming, and that's normal. As healing progresses, slowly those blinders come off and the survivor sees more of the world.

One survivor of rape, a 38 year-old woman, explains it like this:

When all this stuff came screaming back at me, it was like I couldn't look away. I guess that was trauma's way of forcing me to do this incredibly difficult work. As I did the work, the trauma began to slowly fade into the background. It was still on my mind, and of course when I was actively working on it, which I did through therapy and writing in my journal, it was front and center. But when I was with my friends or at work, I could put it aside. It felt like I was waking up from a very long sleep. I suddenly could see beauty in the world that was there all along. That made me feel like my horrible trauma could somehow live alongside all the goodness in the world. They didn't cancel each other out at all, which is how I felt right after I was raped.

Acceptance

An important task in the healing process for survivors of sexual assault and sexual abuse is to accept both the reality of the trauma and its very real effects. Denial and avoidance are normal and pervasive processes in everyone's mental lives. Remember that one trauma effect is intrusion. Intrusive thoughts, flashbacks, nightmares, and rumination thwart our efforts at complete avoidance of contemplating our trauma.

We may need to avoid accepting reality for a time. Eventually, however, our minds will not let past trauma stay buried. When this happens, it is important to work towards acceptance. It's paradoxical, but the more we try to avoid a thought or emotion, to more likely we are to experience it. Researchers have found this in the laboratory, and process-oriented studies of people in therapy also show that those who are more willing to be in touch with their unpleasant thoughts and emotions have better psychological outcomes.[vi] Even before researchers began to measure avoidance, psychologists knew that the starting place for change is acceptance. Famous psychologist Carl Rodgers observed in 1961 that "the curious paradox is that when I accept myself just as I am, *then* I can change" (emphasis mine).[vii]

Acceptance is the starting place for healing. Acceptance of our reality does not equate to approval or resignation. Acceptance does not imply that we are giving up on feeling or acting differently than how we are in the midst of trauma. Acceptance is not passive at all—quite the opposite. Acceptance is an active and brave act. Starting with acceptance brings relief in that we give ourselves permission to feel how we feel. If we have been sexually assaulted, of course we feel upset, or numb, or angry, or scared. Trauma derives it power from secrecy and shame, and looking at our trauma in the light of day, using the correct words and understanding its effects, begins to put us back in control of our lives.

The Person in the Midst of the Pain

Sexual trauma is an action. It's something happens *to* you, not something that you *are*. What happens to us does not define us. What defines us is so much more than that. We are defined by our values, our actions, our attitudes, and our relationships. Although trauma can throw us and make us feel like we are not ourselves, that's only the self in transition. Just as we previously struggled a bit to incorporate new experiences into our lives, such as losing a loved one or changing a career, healing from trauma implies a measure of struggle. Who you are, however, has not changed.

This may be a difficult idea while you are in the midst of trauma effects. You may feel like you don't have control of your thoughts and emotions, or see yourself as a weaker version of yourself. It's understandable to feel this way, but the person you were before the assault is still there, deep down.

It can be very helpful when healing from trauma to engage in activities that remind us of who we are. Anything that allows you to feel more like yourself is a good use of your time and energy. I've seen survivors re-engage in old activities like playing a favorite sport or returning to an absorbing hobby. Some re-read favorite books, or research a favorite subject. Make efforts to give yourself experiences that remind you that you are more than your trauma, and you are bigger than your pain. I like to remind my clients that they can get burned out on therapy work, and it's important to be involved in activities that are enjoyable and not related to trauma in any way.

Survivors Speak- Sabrina, Age 53

I got divorced five years ago. About one year after my

divorce, I felt ready to pursue a new relationship. I really wanted a new partner in my life and wanted to start over. I met a man at a friend's party and he seemed nice. We went out on a few dates and things seemed to be going well. I told him that I was recently divorced and wasn't ready to be intimate. He seemed okay with that at first, but he slowly began to pressure me to have sex. One night after a date I was over at his house and he forced himself on me. I told him to stop, but he just kept going. I didn't want to have sex, but he raped me.

I was in shock for a while, and in reality I was in denial. I didn't call it rape, but I knew that I had been violated. I stopped talking to the guy, wanting to block it all out. I retreated from the dating world, and from my family and friends. I blamed myself for what happened. I felt so stupid and ashamed, like I should have known better.

I couldn't forget about what happened. I noticed that I was spiraling downward. I was comfort-eating and not sleeping. I kept having nightmares about the rape. I felt afraid all the time, and experienced intense anxiety. I knew I had to treat this seriously. After my divorce, I learned I had to treat it like a loss and grieve. With the rape, I had to do the same thing. I accepted that it happened, and tried to move forward.

I wasn't sure how to start, but I did some reading and started with the basics. I got my diet under control and started going to the gym again. I tired myself out with exercise and *that helped me to get more sleep. I told some close friends what happened. They were very supportive. Even though I didn't know exactly what I needed at the time, they let me know they were there for me. I didn't feel safe in my bed, so I started sleeping in the guest room. It seemed silly, but it really helped in the beginning and made me feel safe.*

I found a therapist that I clicked with and I began the difficult work of processing through all those horrible memories and scary feelings. For me, this also was a process of acceptance. I had this idea that if I didn't allow the sadness or anger or shame to come up, then I wouldn't have to face what really happened. But once I let myself feel, I slowly started to notice changes. I felt safer and less anxious. The intrusive thoughts decreased. I remembered that I am a whole person with a whole life, not just a victim who is surviving day to day.

It's been a difficult journey but it does get better. To other survivors I would say that emotions are key. As cliché as it sounds, you need to feel your feelings, and they won't last forever. Staying in denial doesn't give you control over your life. In a way, it's giving control over to the abuser, since their actions prevent you from living as a whole person. Take you power back. Feeling is not a weakness, it's a strength.

Chapter 9: The Option of Therapy

Psychotherapy is certainly not the only tool for recovery from sexual trauma, but it is an important part of many survivors' healing process. The idea of psychotherapy can be a scary prospect, especially if you have never met with a therapist. Even if you have done therapy work before, going to a therapist specifically for trauma can be daunting. In this chapter I will outline what psychotherapy for trauma looks like, and provide some guidance about how to pick a competent and caring therapist to partner with you on your journey.

Trauma Therapy is Effective

The first point I'd like to emphasize in our discussion about trauma therapy is its effectiveness. PTSD, the most common diagnosis for survivors of sexual assault, is a very treatable issue and the majority of people fully recover. Many survivors don't fit into the PTSD diagnosis, but still benefit greatly from therapy.

There are different approaches to trauma therapy but all evidence-based therapies for sexual trauma are effective. However, some approaches may be better for certain people than others. Later in this chapter I will outline some evidence-based models for trauma treatment, as well as discuss what may fit for you. Regardless of the model, however, all good therapy is characterized by some core features.

Your therapist should, first and foremost, be accepting and non-judgmental. He or she should be aware of the myths and facts around sexual assault, and should make you feel comfortable and not blamed in any way. In order to do therapy work, you need to be able to be vulnerable, and that's impossible in an environment of judgment or criticism.

Finding a therapist can be like finding a good doctor; when you have a specific issue that needs work, you search for a specialist. Seek out someone who has expertise in the issue that's at hand. It's appropriate to ask potential therapists about their training or experience working with survivors of sexual assault. Trauma is a different animal, so to speak, and it's crucial to partner with someone who understands the nuances of trauma and is well-versed in trauma treatment. A few examples of initial questions to ask are:

- Have you worked with survivors of sexual assault before?
- Do you have any special training or certificates in trauma treatment?
- Do you consider yourself an expert in trauma therapy?
- Do you think that anyone set themselves up for sexual

assault by drinking or using drugs, or being in dangerous places?

- How do you usually help a survivor of sexual assault?

When psychiatry was born, all therapists practiced within a medical model. Mental health practitioners searched for and diagnosed pathology in their patients, and then set about treating them. More current thinking takes a *nonpathologizing* approach. In other words, therapists look for the function of their client's symptoms, and assume that even self-destructive behaviors and symptoms serve some sort of purpose and are helping someone cope with upsetting thoughts or behaviors.

A nonpathologizing viewpoint is especially crucial in the realm of trauma treatment. Just as we explored common trauma effects earlier in this book, your therapist should be able to view your particular struggles as your body and mind's way of coping after an assault, not a marker of mental illness. Your therapist should view any symptoms you have as a normal response to trauma, not pathology.

Effective trauma therapy should also be empowering. As we discussed earlier, it's crucial for sexual assault survivors to have control handed back to them, since it was taken away during the assault. In the relationship between therapist and client, there can often be a power imbalance. The therapist is seen as the expert in the room, and the client is there to listen and take advice. Effective therapists, however, realize that you are always the expert on you, no matter how many degrees are on the therapists' walls. Therapists that seek to empower their clients encourage open communication and feedback, and they welcome discussions about what's not working in therapy or what is simply not feasible.

If you feel that your therapist is not listening to you, or not empowering you to take control of your healing process, it's time to think about ending that relationship. It's true that part of the therapists' role in trauma work is to gently push their clients to the edge of their comfort zone in order to process uncomfortable memories and emotions. However, if there is no room for you, as the client, to direct this process, therapy can feel re-traumatizing.

Going hand in hand with empowerment, good trauma therapy is collaborative. Your therapist does have knowledge that you don't, but he or she should also collaborate with you to plan how sessions will look, what your goals are, and how you will reach those goals together. As a therapist, I have a plethora of techniques and tools that can help my clients, but each individual is unique. I've learned that survivors are intuitive and creative in their own process, and they often have better ideas about what's helpful than I do. I don't view my role as one where I hand down wisdom and dictate how to go about healing. I view myself as a partner in the process, a fellow traveler on this difficult road. I learn as much from my clients as they learn from me. Make sure that you feel you are collaborating with your therapist, and don't be afraid to speak up about what works best for you.

Survivors have had their most intimate boundaries violently violated. Therefore, boundaries are extremely important in trauma therapy. It's your therapist's responsibility to hold professional boundaries, and clearly explain those boundaries. In all of our other relationships, it's a two-way street of sharing and support. But in therapy, the relationship is one-way. This means that it's not appropriate for your therapist to overly share about his or her life or feelings. They are there to support you, and it's not your responsibility to worry about them. It's normal for trauma survivors to sometimes feel guilty when they share about their assault with friends or family, worrying that they are being a "burden" or upsetting others. In therapy, it can be a relief to talk with someone who will not be upset or overwhelmed by your story. A therapist who specializes in trauma will have heard many people's stories, and already has good support in place in order to do this challenging work. Examples of unhealthy boundaries in therapy are:

- Physical contact (exemptions might include a hug if

it's first talked about and agreed to)

- Too much self-disclosure from the therapist (especially about the therapist's own issues)

- Not being clear about the structure of therapy (how often you meet for sessions, how absences are handled, etc.)

- Therapist using sessions to work on his or her own problems

- Therapist having a dual role in your life (for example, being both your therapist and your babysitter)

- Therapist approaching you outside of your sessions (the rule for encountering your therapist in public is that it's up to you to first initiate contact if you choose; this respects your confidentiality as a client)

Boundary violations of this kind are very rare, but if there is anything your therapist says or does that makes you uncomfortable, it's always appropriate to speak about it with them.

In addition to holding safe boundaries, effective trauma therapists work hard to create an atmosphere of transparency in their work with clients. Being open and clear helps empower survivors and puts them in the driver's seat when it comes to their own healing. When working with a therapist, you should always understand your role and what's expected of you. You should also understand your therapist's role and what you can expect of him or her. Your therapist should have open dialogue about the process of trauma therapy, and they should clearly explain any psychological terms that they use. You should feel comfortable asking questions of your therapist, and feel that there will be no repercussions if you disagree with him or her.

Laying a Good Foundation

If you have never been to therapy before, it's hard to know what to expect. Even if you have been to therapy in the past, it's difficult to know what therapy for sexual assault looks like.

Effective trauma therapy works in stages, just like the healing process. Trauma therapy begins with creating safety and re-regulating yourself so that you can cope with any trauma effects and have a strong base from which to begin slowly delving into the trauma itself. In therapy, creating safety includes becoming comfortable with your therapist, asking questions and getting clear answers, and slowly increasing your ability to be vulnerable in a therapy session. It's important to create a good foundation with your therapist so that this vulnerability can happen. By vulnerability, I mean the ability to be open and honest with your therapist about what you think and feel, and the feeling that it is safe enough for you to feel your emotions fully in their presence. In summary, the beginning stage of trauma therapy involves creating safety by building rapport, being informed about the course of therapy, and slowly letting our guards down with a trusted person.

Once you've worked with a therapist to create trust and safety, work begins toward re-regulation and learning new coping skills. As we've learned, trauma de-regulates our bodies and minds. An effective trauma therapist will work with you to find the best tools to utilize for coping with the effects of trauma. This might include using grounding during a flashback, working with compassion and positive self-talk when in the midst of shame, or helping you be accountable for cultivating healthy habits for eating, sleeping, and exercise. Regulation also includes using our rational minds to put a name to our thoughts and feelings and recognize trauma effects for what they are.

Telling the Story, Mourning the Loss

After safety and regulation are established and you feel confident in your ability to cope in difficult moments, therapy work may turn to the second stage: remembrance and mourning. With a therapist, this may include telling the story of your assault, and exploring all of the emotions and physical sensations that come with speaking your truth. Your therapist might prompt you with questions such as: "What happened next?" or "What did that feel like for you?" Your therapist will help you regulate yourself in the moment while you recount your experience, helping you use your tools if you need them to remain centered and present.

For most survivors, this part of therapy is the most difficult. My clients often tell me that it's the part they most dread. One survivor I worked with put it this way:

I knew this day would come. I feel like this is the most important thing to tell you, what actually happened to me. At the same time, it's the scariest thing to say out loud. Saying it out loud somehow makes it more real. Finding the words is hard. I am scared about what you [the therapist] will think, and what I'll have to acknowledge about my life. I'm afraid of all the emotions that I've been running from.

Revisiting memories in this way with a therapist is sometimes called Prolonged Exposure Therapy, because the survivor is intentionally exposing themselves to painful memories and difficult emotions, and they do so more than once. As you recount your story in a safe environment, it begins to lose its ability to make you panic or shut down.

Although a rape will never be a "normal" event in someone's life, revisiting trauma does have a normalizing effect. The memories begin to point not to a current emergency, but to a painful and tragic event that happened in the past. You will find you can talk about your own trauma without paralyzing anxiety or crippling sadness. As we put language to our experience, we begin the organizing process in our brains, and the trauma begins to rest in our past, where it belongs.

Doing exposure work is hard but effective. Research has shown that this kind of therapy, if it's right for the individual survivor, is the most effective for reducing trauma symptoms.[i] Prolonged Exposure Therapy is a recommended treatment supported by the International Society for Traumatic Stress Studies.

You may decide with your therapist that exploring the past in this way is not necessary or helpful in your process. If this is the case, therapy work in the second stage focuses on mourning the past without re-visiting it. There may be exposure work in the sense that your therapist will help you experience uncomfortable thoughts and emotions that are related to sexual trauma.

Integration and Solidifying Gains

After doing exposure work, trauma effects and other

symptoms usually begin to subside. Revisiting the trauma and tolerating distressing thoughts and emotions have taken the sting out of intrusive memories. In the final stage of trauma therapy, you work with your therapist to integrate the assault into the rest of your life. Your therapist will help you to create a new narrative about your trauma, one that acknowledges the tragedy and pain of loss, but also points to your strength and empowerment.

It's normal even in the final stage of therapy to have occasional "flare-ups" of symptoms. Often, survivors feel that they are losing their gains or winding up back at square one. However, most survivors at this stage can use tools learned in therapy to re-regulate themselves, can use compassionate self-talk to avoid beating themselves up, and find that these symptoms are temporary. In this stage of treatment gains made in healing are never lost and coping skills are always available to you, even if it's difficult to access them in the moment. In the face of an unexpected trauma effect, we all need to go back to basics.

In this stage of treatment survivors usually begin to grapple with the meaning of trauma in their lives. In order for full integration to happen, we need to do the seemingly impossible; we need to fit the reality of sexual assault into our broader worldview or system of meaning. I've seen survivors find solace in their newfound strengths, and while they admit they would not choose this difficult path, they honor the growth they have had through the healing process. Other survivors note how their relationships have deepened and taken on a new intimacy because they reached out for support. Others utilize their faith systems to create meaning. During this process, your therapist can reflect your strengths, be a sounding board, and support you.

The ending of therapy can be difficult. This decision should be made in collaboration with your therapist. It's normal to feel ambivalent about ending therapy. On the one hand, survivors reflect that they are excited to move forward on their own and to be free of a regular reminder of their trauma. On the other hand, there is valid anxiety and trepidation about losing the structure and support of therapy, as well as losing a relationship that has become special.

Sometimes therapists taper off therapy with survivors, meeting less frequently over time. Winding down in this way is a good strategy to ease into life without therapy. While ending therapy, it's also important to spend time processing the feelings that come with good-byes. I always spend time talking openly about how to say good-bye, and I make sure to reflect all of the progress the survivor has made, and I point out the strengths they have that will serve them well in the future.

Progress Does Not Equal Feeling Better—At Least, Not At First

Survivors come to therapy for one reason: they want to feel better. This is a valid and understandable reason for seeking any kind of help. While trauma therapy is very effective, I also take pains to explain that therapy for sexual trauma necessarily involves exploring and experiencing difficult thoughts, feelings, and memories. In short, it feels worse before it feels better. It's important to avoid measuring your own progress in healing with how you feel day-to-day. Just like a good exercise program, if you are comfortable all the time you may not be progressing towards your goals.

Your sessions with your therapist should not be overwhelming, but also should not always be easy. Although the pace of therapy is always in your control, part of the therapist's role is to gently challenge you and go with you to the edge of your comfort zone. Sometimes, they invite you to take a step outside that comfort zone and face something very scary. This is a tall order, but in your session you are never alone or without help.

What Type of Therapy is Right for Me?

Although there are common elements in effective

trauma therapy, including non-judgment, support, education, and using exposure (when appropriate), there are different approaches to psychotherapy for sexual assault. Here I will review several more common types of therapy, and outline who might benefit the most from each one.

Logical Thinkers and Cognitive-Behavioral Therapy (CBT)

Cognitive-Behavioral Therapy (CBT) was first developed in the 1970s to treat depression as a blend of Cognitive Therapy and Behavior Therapy. In this context, the term cognitive simply refers to thoughts or thinking. CBT therapists focus on the connections between our thoughts, our feelings, and our behaviors. In CBT, therapists work with their clients to identify specific thoughts or thinking patterns that make them upset, afraid, or guilty.

Therapists then examine these thoughts with clients and try to replace them with more positive or adaptive thoughts. For example, thoughts around the assault such as "I must have deserved that" or "I should not have put myself in that situation" are gently challenged by the therapist and replaced with thoughts such as "no one deserves to be raped" or "it wasn't my fault." As our thoughts begin to change, so do our feelings and behaviors. In the realm of sexual assault, CBT will usually include doing exposure work, and focus on soothing self-talk for regulation while telling the story of the trauma.

CBT is an evidence-based treatment for PTSD. In a large review of the research on CBT, the International Society for Traumatic Stress Studies concluded that the evidence for its effectiveness is "compelling," with many studies reflecting a significant decrease in symptoms.[ii]

CBT works well for people who are logical thinkers, and who tend to experience most of their distress in their minds and thoughts, rather than in their bodies. If you find yourself to be an intellectualizer and are often "in your head," CBT would be a good choice for you because of its emphasis on rationality and examining thoughts. Additionally, CBT will be a good choice for a survivor who has experienced a relatively recent assault, as negative thinking patterns may be less ingrained than for a survivor of childhood sexual abuse.

A Look Inside: Psychodynamic Therapy

Psychodynamic therapy is the modern extension of the classical psychoanalysis that Freud practiced. Today's psychodynamic therapy, however, does not necessarily include lying down on a couch or having a therapist that does not interact with you. There are seven core features that define psychodynamic therapy:[iii]

1. A focus on emotions and expression of emotion in the moment

In contrast to CBT, where the focus is on the expression of thoughts, psychodynamic therapy focuses on the expression of emotions. The therapist helps you identify and explore emotions, especially when the feelings are contradictory, troubling, distressing, or difficult to recognize or acknowledge.

2. Exploration of avoidance

In psychodynamic therapy, the therapist helps their clients recognize how they avoid uncomfortable thoughts and feelings, and what this avoidance might mean for them. The therapist helps the client know their demons and slowly begin to stand up to them.

3. Identification of recurring themes and patterns

There is a saying in psychodynamic therapy that "whatever you are doing is working for you." This means that even patterns that on the surface look self-defeating serve an important psychological purpose, such as when a survivor finds themselves in relationships that mirror early abuse. Psychodynamic therapists help their clients identify and explore patterns in their lives. If warranted, the therapist will help with changing these patterns.

4. Analysis of past experience

Psychodynamic therapists see present behaviors, feelings, and thoughts as connected to past experiences. In psychodynamic therapy, a therapist may help you to understand how your past experience shapes how you view the world today.

5. Focus on relationships

In psychodynamic therapy, there is an emphasis on exploring relationship patterns, both with others and with the self. Therapists see relationships in terms of how someone is getting their emotional needs met. In therapy, work is done on relationships to help clients have healthy boundaries and get all their needs met in a healthy way.

6. Emphasis on the therapy relationship

Because relationships are so important in a psychodynamic view, the relationship between the therapist and the client is fertile ground for exploring interpersonal patterns in the here-and-now. Any relationship pattern in a person's life is, to some extent, repeated with the therapist. Since therapy is an open and safe space, it's an opportunity to verbalize the feelings we have about another person that we usually edit due to social norms. For example, a client can tell the therapist that they feel angry with them, or disappointed, or abandoned, and they can be heard in a non-defensive way.

A client I worked with who is a survivor of childhood sexual abuse had struggled her whole life with being a "people pleaser" and she noticed she wanted my approval as well. Since my role as a therapist was more neutral (neither approving nor disapproving of her thoughts and feelings) than she was used to, she found herself trying to "please" me. As I noticed this pattern I gently brought it into the open, and she was able to verbalize how her approval-seeking was related to her trauma history, and she was able to tolerate not getting approval for her own internal experiences. She expressed to me that she had always felt "what I thought and felt was wrong in some way, and I needed someone else to tell me it's okay." As we worked together, she began to have more confidence in her own internal experience and she noticed less "people pleasing" behavior in her other relationships.

7. Exploration and validation of fantasy life

In psychodynamic therapy, value is placed on a client's internal mental life, which includes private daydreams, fantasies, or dreams while asleep. Psychodynamic therapists see this unedited mental activity as rich ground for understanding how someone sees themselves, others, and the world around them.

Studies of psychodynamic therapy show that it proves to be just as effective as CBT for a wide variety of issues. In-depth analyses of psychodynamic therapy find an effect size of around 0.80.[iv] An effect size is a number that captures how much a particular treatment changes someone's symptoms. In psychological and medical research, an effect size of 0.2 is considered small, an effect size of 0.5 is moderate, and a large effect size is 0.80.

Psychodynamic therapy may be especially helpful for survivors of childhood sexual abuse, due to its focus on the past and relationship patterns. This kind of therapy might also appeal to someone who experiences themselves as a "feeler" rather than a "thinker" and is interested in a deeper exploration of their thoughts and emotions.

Re-setting the Brain: Eye Movement Desensitization and Reprocessing (EMDR)

Eye Movement Desensitization and Reprocessing (EMDR) is a relatively new way to conduct an exposure-based therapy. It was developed in the late 1980s specifically to treat trauma, and it focuses on helping clients with intrusive and distressing thoughts, feelings, and images related to their trauma. The core idea behind EMDR treatment is that when trauma occurs, it overwhelms our normal coping mechanisms (both in our minds and bodies). Due to this overload the traumatic event is not processed in a normal way, and the traumatic memory (with associated stimuli like sights, sounds, smells, thoughts, and feelings) is stored in an isolated memory network. The goal of EMDR is to re-process these memories so that they become more integrated with the rest of our memories, and are more adaptable to new information.

EMDR relies on the combination of our minds and our bodies. In EMDR sessions, a client recalls trauma-based memories while receiving bodily stimuli that are bilateral, meaning some kind of touch or sight that includes both sides of our bodies. This can happen by tapping alternately on each hand, or moving the eyes from side to side. Sometimes a therapist will move his or her finger, and ask the client to follow it with their eyes. Sometimes a light board is used, and the client follows the light. If the client is comfortable with touch, the therapist might tap on their hands.

EMDR has been shown to be an effective treatment for PTSD and for survivors of sexual trauma in particular, with 75% of rape survivors no longer meeting the criteria for PTSD after utilizing EMDR with an EMDR-certified therapist.[v]

EMDR is often combined with psychodynamic therapy and/or CBT. EMDR is a good choice for survivors who are struggling with intrusive symptoms, and who are drawn to a highly structured type of therapy.

Strength in Numbers: Group Therapy

Group therapy is different from individual therapy in several ways. The most obvious is that therapy is done in a group of survivors, with one or two therapists facilitating. There are always ground rules for groups that help with cohesiveness and appropriate boundaries. Groups may be highly structured, with specific topics for discussion and group exercises, or they may be less structured with more time for open discussion for member-generated topics. Groups can also be a combination of structured time and unstructured time.

Many survivors find the prospect of group therapy frightening, and understandably so. Getting together with relative strangers to share your thoughts and feelings about your trauma can be daunting. However, group therapy is powerful because you can be vulnerable and honest in a safe space with others who understand what you are struggling with. It is empowering to say out loud something that you previously denied, pushed away, or were embarrassed about. Many survivors who take that leap look around the room and, for the first time in their lives, see understanding faces nodding vigorously in agreement. Being in a group can drastically reduce a survivor's feelings of isolation, alienation, or estrangement.

Research shows the group therapy is just as effective as individual therapy and leads to significant decreases in trauma-related symptoms.[vi] Groups offer unique opportunities to explore how you relate to others, receive honest feedback, and discover your similarities with others survivors. The effects of trauma thrive in secret. A group allows you to explore these effects in the open, and to hear from others how they experience you.

Group therapy is often combined with individual therapy, and this can be a very effective approach. Group therapy is a good choice for survivors who want to connect with other survivors, or who struggle with guilt and shame surrounding their trauma.

What about Medication?

Medication for mental disorders remains a controversial issue. Ultimately, it will be up to you and your doctor (if you consult one) to decide if medication is right for you. There is well-supported evidence that a trauma like sexual assault, and its resulting effects or symptoms, are a direct result of dysfunction at the level of the brain.[vii] In Chapter 4 we explored these imbalances and abnormalities. Psychiatric medications are designed to address these imbalances by either inhibiting or boosting certain neurotransmitters. In this way, psychiatric medications are exactly like any other medication. For example, if someone has asthma, they may take a drug that acts on systems in the lungs to help them breathe better. The brain is an organ, and it can be dysregulated just like any other organ. Medications can, at times, help to re-regulate our brain which helps with symptoms like anxiety and hyperarousal.

Psychiatric medications work to mitigate symptoms and cannot be a substitute for the hard work of integrating a trauma into your life narrative. Medications, however, facilitate the healing process by returning survivors to a higher level of functioning by controlling trauma effects such as depressed mood, anxiety, panic attacks, and difficulty sleeping.

An informed use of medications can help a survivor to heal like they might recover from a car accident. If someone is in an accident and breaks their shoulder, they need to do physical therapy in order to fully heal. Physical therapy is difficult and is impossible if the patient is in too much pain. In this example, the patient may take medication to control their pain and allow them to do the stretches and exercises that are necessary for a full recovery. The pain medication itself does not equal recovery; it's just a tool to facilitate the recovery process. Psychiatric medications function in the same way. They help regulate mood and general functioning to allow a survivor to tolerate the work they do for their healing. In fact, there is strong evidence that the best outcomes for people struggling with PTSD are a combination of both medication and some kind of talk therapy (like the ones outlined earlier in this chapter).[viii]

Psychiatric medications can be prescribed by a psychiatrist (an MD with a specialty in psychiatry), your primary care physician, or a nurse practitioner with special certifications. It's best to consult a psychiatrist or a psychiatric nurse practitioner, if possible. These two groups have considerable training in psychiatric conditions and specifically work with these types of medications. Primary care physicians, on the other hand, are typically generalists and have less training in mental health. Some primary care physicians do not prescribe psychiatric medications as a rule and will refer you to a psychiatrist. More important than any degree or training, however, is finding a provider that you feel comfortable with, and who will partner with you in your healing process. Here are some suggested questions to ask your provider when exploring medication:

- How will this medication help me?

- What are the side effects, if any?
- How will I work up to the therapeutic dose?
- If I decide to stop this medication, can I stop it all at once, or do I need to taper off?
- How will we know if the medication if working? What if we need to adjust the dose?
- Do I take this medication daily, or only when I feel anxious/depressed/panicked?

You are in Control

What kind of therapy to use and whether to explore medication is up to you. In trauma, we are not in control. In healing, we must be. Educating yourself about your options and choosing your helpers wisely can vastly improve your healing process. Take time to learn about therapy and meet with several therapists until you feel safe and comfortable. With medications, take time to advocate for yourself and get all of your questions answered. The right partners in your healing process will make you feel safe and heard while also gently challenging you and helping you to move past your trauma.

Survivors Speak- Cassandra, Age 25

I think the hardest part of therapy for me was actually admitting I needed help. I was still functioning okay 2 years after I was raped, but life just seemed to keep getting harder. I was noticing new symptoms, or maybe I just lost my ability to ignore them.

I had been to two therapists before. One was when I was in high school and my parents were getting a divorce. I don't remember having a particularly difficult time, but I think they wanted me to have someone to talk to. I remember it feeling awkward, and I only went for a few weeks before begging my parents to let me drop it. Later, when I was in college, I saw a counselor at the student health center because I felt depressed. It was still a little awkward but I felt understood. After about two months I felt less depressed and decided to end the therapy. The therapist agreed with me, and could see that I had made progress.

For me, deciding to reach out for help around the rape itself felt much more daunting than getting help for depression in college. Something in me knew it would be harder. My boyfriend was very supportive and encouraged me to call someone. After one really bad day, I was crying and feeling so panicked and I knew I needed some kind of help.

*I contacted a few people and had meetings with them.
I wanted to feel a connection with someone before telling my
whole story. I ended up working with a trauma specialist, and
it is true that they say it feels worse before it feels better. I like
to think of it like a surgery. Of course a surgery doesn't feel
good, but it does wonders for you in the long run.*

*First we focused on simply getting me back to my
normal self. By normal I mean the girl that can go to work and
do a good job, has good relationships, and feels generally
stable. At first I was surprised by the simplicity of my
therapist's suggestions, but I hadn't realized how I had let the
little things slide because I was trying to survive my day.
Things like eating regular meals, getting some good sleep, and
re-connecting with my running shoes went a long way. I also
got some coping tools under my belt to deal with the really
hard days.*

*One thing I didn't anticipate getting in the beginning
of therapy was a new (and helpful) vocabulary to describe my
experience. I had some words and concepts to help me wrap
my mind around what was really happening to me. For the
first time, I could explain to my boyfriend how I felt and why I
felt that way. This alone was extremely helpful.*

*The next part of therapy was the hardest. I had to
really open up and talk about what happened. Dredging up the
details was very painful, and I felt so exposed in my therapy*

sessions. My therapist was kind, understanding, and supportive, but it was still so hard. I had spent two years building up emotional barriers and she was slowly taking them down.

Slowly, things began to shift. As I talked about it over and over, I felt less panicked and depressed about it. It's hard to put into words, but it sort of faded into the background. I felt heard and listened to. I remember my therapist just looking at me one day and saying, "I'm so sorry that happened to you." I cried really hard that day, and it actually felt good.

I learned that I could tolerate so much more than I thought I could. I learned to not be afraid of my feelings. I don't enjoy feeling sad or anxious, but I sure can sit with them until it passes over me like a wave. I learned about the darker side of my personality, and explored it with a supportive and accepting person that I respected. I'm proud of myself that I stuck with therapy even when it was hard.

There were many weeks when I walked into my therapist's office and announced, "I don't want to be here today." She would just nod nicely and say, "That's fair. I've been known to ruin good moods. But since you're here, let's do some work." On good days that made me laugh and on bad days I just breathed through it.

Therapy is hard, but it's really worth it. You are worth it, and your well-being is worth it. Healing is possible.

Chapter Ten: Tools for Healing

In this chapter, we will explore some concrete skills for coping with trauma effects. These tools will be useful in your healing process. I've divided them into two categories: external tools and internal tools. External tools are those that deal with our environment and behaviors. Internal tools refer to work that we do internally in the realm of our thoughts or emotions.

External Tools

The Big Three (Diet, Exercise, and Sleep)

In Chapter 4 we explored how trauma leads to dysregulation of brain and body systems. The first step in healing is to hit the reset button and return to self-regulation. I like to focus on what I call The Big Three as a starting place for regulation. Trauma tends to throw us off balance in almost all of our routines, and our sleeping, eating, and moving is no exception. An important tool for healing is to be mindful of diet, exercise, and sleep habits. You know yourself better than anyone, and you know how to fit healthy food, some movement, and time for rest into your daily routine. For more specific tips, refer to Chapter 4.

Creating Structure

For trauma survivors, free time can feel scary. Our unoccupied minds might wheel off into anxious worrying, or ruminating depression, or we may circle around and around the memories of the assault. Adding structure to your day can help ward off unhelpful thought patterns and can also help regulate emotion. Having structure can also prevent impulsivity. We all get a little lift in our mood when we are productive and use our time wisely, either to tackle the to-do list or to intentionally engage in pleasurable activities.

Keep a calendar and write down your appointments for work hours. Notice large gaps of free time and make a plan for those times. Be mindful of your need for both activity and down-time. You might pick up a new hobby or return to an old one. Having a sense of mastery in our lives is important when we are healing. This could be as simple as cooking a new recipe or complicated as learning a new instrument. Remember to plan for self-care activities like regular meals, exercise, and sleep.

Creating Safety

In the external sense, safety is created by being intentional about our environments. Survivors of sexual trauma have a high need for predictability and a sense of safety in their homes. If you find yourself not feeling safe in your home or at work, you can take steps to increase your sense of security. This may mean asking a co-worker to walk you to your car after work, or setting up a phone call at that time with a supportive friend or family member. You may add a security system to your home, or take a friend with you when you walk your dog. Some survivors bring in a safety object to work and put it on their desks, such as a picture of loved ones. You may ask your roommate or spouse to let you know they are on the way home before arriving and opening the door. Pets can be both a comfort and add a sense of safety to a home. Don't be afraid to ask for what you need or to get creative.

Support Systems

Our relationships can uplift us like nothing else can. When healing from a sexual assault, take care to create and attend to a good support system. Reaching out to others comes easily to some people, and for others it's a challenge. Your support system can catch you when you fall, remind you of your strengths, and simply be there when you need to talk. Your family and friends can also act as a feedback system for you. They can reflect on your progress and stuck points. Good friends and close family sometimes know what we need even before we do, whether it's encouragement or a nudge toward more healthy behaviors.

You are always in control of what you share with people. You may choose to disclose that you were sexually assaulted, and are doing the hard work of healing from trauma. You may choose to simply say that you are going through a hard time in your life and may call on them for extra support. Be prepared for your family and friends to be curious about what is going on with you, but remember that your life is private, and you can set boundaries around what you are ready to share.

It's also important to ask for what you need at work or in school, if that feels safe for you. It's up to you what you want to disclose, and you can always ask for some extra support and not name a specific reason. Explore your employer's policies for leave or flexible hours to allow you time for therapy and rest. If you are in school, see your guidance counselor or student resource center.

Internal Tools

Grounding

Grounding is a psychological tool that aims to help us be in the present moment, feel centered, and regulate our emotions. Grounding is a general term, and someone can use grounding in a lot of different ways. You can think of grounding as having at least one foot firmly on the ground so we don't get too carried away. For sexual assault survivors, grounding is especially helpful because it helps prevent us from dissociating too much or losing ourselves in past memories. In either case, we are not grounded in the present, but off somewhere else, either reliving the past or disconnecting from our present experience.

Grounding does not mean that we deny what we are feeling in favor of a calm, Zen-like state. Grounding means that we are present with our experience, whatever it is, but we feel centered and rooted in our body. Usually, our emotions become overwhelming because we are reliving the past or projecting ourselves into the future.

Take anxiety, for example. While grounding, we notice that we feel anxious, but also can feel our breath and focus on the present. My internal dialogue would go something like this: *I notice I'm feeling anxious. There's that tight feeling in my chest and I'm thinking about what scary thing is around the corner. I'll try not going with those thoughts, and stay right here. Focus on my breathing, in and out. I don't need to think about the past or future right now, just to be right here and breathe through this.*

Notice that grounding feels very different than having anxiety trigger anxious thoughts about what could happen in the future. Before we know it, our mind is zooming in a million directions as we imagine all the disasters in our future. Moving our focus away from the present amplifies anxiety. Using grounding, however, can keep us anchored even as we notice some anxious feelings.

Grounding is especially helpful for flashbacks and intrusive thoughts about the sexual assault itself. Since trauma memories are not processed fully, they come popping up at us and it feels as if the assault is happening again. Thoughts about the assault and flashbacks can trigger the emotions that would come if we were really in danger, such as panic. When this happens, it's vital to remain grounded because then we can realize the truth: that we are not in danger in the present, but having a thought about the past. Staying rooted in the present interrupts flashbacks and rumination cycles.

There are three main ways of grounding: mental, physical, and soothing.

Mental Grounding

Mental grounding refers to using your mind to focus on the present. The easiest way to do this is to describe your surroundings in detail, either out loud or in your mind. Describe the objects around you, their sizes and colors and textures. You can describe the temperature around you, how your clothes feel on your body, and any smells you notice. Try to have a non-judgmental stance; you are simply observing. This forces your mind into the present as you name objects around you and notice all the details about the here-and-now.

You can use this simple script for mental grounding:

I am here at _____

The time is _____, the day is _____

Three objects I notice around me are_____

Three colors I notice around me are _____

Three textures I notice around me are _____

My body feels _____

Three sounds I can hear are _____

Physical Grounding

Physical grounding engages our sense of touch to bring us into the present, and to help us connect with our environment in a real, physical way. We rarely focus on our sense of touch. As we go about our day, our mind wisely puts all kinds of physical sensations into the background. For instance, we rarely are aware of how our clothes feel on our body. If we were aware of every texture, every heaviness, every shift in fabric, it would be difficult to accomplish anything. We can, however, focus on our sense of touch as a grounding tool. Because a physical object is immediate and concrete, using physical touch can root us in the present.

Some examples of physical grounding are:

- Take off your shoes. Feel the ground beneath you. Feel your toes and heel root to the ground. Notice the texture and temperature of the earth or floor.
- Walk slowly in a quiet place. Feel your body's movements as you move through space.
- Run warm or cold water over your hands. Notice the changes in temperature and how the water feels on your skin.
- Carry a small, smooth stone with you to use as a grounding object. Take it out and hold it in your hand when you need to be centered. Feel the texture and weight of the rock, and know that you are in the present moment.
- Roll Chinese Medicine Balls in your palm.
- Keep a small bottle of your favorite lotion with you. Use it when you are feeling overwhelmed. Focus only on the sensation of the lotion on your skin.

Soothing Grounding

Soothing grounding includes a variety of techniques aimed at self-soothing. Soothing ourselves in difficult moments can help turn down the volume of difficult thoughts and emotions. When we are grounded and soothed, we can be calmer and have more rational and compassionate thoughts about ourselves.

Examples of soothing grounding techniques are:

- Say a kind statement to yourself, such as "I am having a normal reaction to an abnormal situation" or "I can breathe through this."
- Remember the words to an uplifting song or quote.
- Plan a treat for yourself in the future, such as a favorite meal or small purchase.
- Think of 3 things that you are grateful for.
- Hug a pillow.

Emotion Regulation

Similar to grounding, emotion regulation is a tool to help you stay centered in the midst of trauma effects. Although we can't completely control our emotions, it's important to feel like we can cope effectively with uncomfortable emotions.

The goal of emotion regulation is not to completely avoid certain emotions, but to manage them. This may mean learning to downshift certain very intense emotions, or to slightly detach from them. Emotion regulation skills increase our ability to acknowledge and then let go of distressing emotions so we do not act from a place of intense sadness or anger or anxiety.

An effective framework for emotion regulation can be found in Dialectical Behavior Therapy (DBT)[i] and includes three core skills:

1. Understanding emotions
2. Reducing emotional vulnerability
3. Decreasing emotional suffering

Understanding Emotions

The first skill focuses on naming and understanding different emotions, with an emphasis on a non-judgmental stance towards one's own emotions. The emotions of survivors can feel like a minefield, ready to explode at any time. It's amazing how much more control we feel over our emotions when we simply find the correct names for them. With this skill, we move from simply identifying "feeling bad" or "feeling good" to using specific terms like "anxious," "irritable," "nervous," and "afraid." In therapy, you may work with your therapist to help you grow your vocabulary of emotions and recognize how these emotions manifest in your thoughts, feelings, and physical sensations. On your own, it can be helpful to keep a list of emotion words with you that you can reference and use to begin to recognize familiar feeling states.

Another important part of understanding emotions is the concept of primary and secondary emotions. A *primary emotion* is an initial reaction to an event, either internal or external. It might be a reaction to a trigger. The primary emotion is always our first knee-jerk response. A *secondary emotion* is a reaction to our primary emotion; it's how we feel about our knee-jerk response. For example, if you encounter a trigger in your day, you might immediately feel fear because that trigger is linked with the fear you experienced during the assault. After you notice the fear, you might become angry with yourself, thinking, "That guy is not the attacker; you're so stupid. You're always jumping at the sight of every guy with dark hair. Just stop it!" In this example, fear is the primary emotion and anger is the secondary emotion.

You can see that a secondary emotion is caused by how we judge our primary emotions. If we take a non-judgmental stance toward our primary emotions, simply accepting them as they are and being compassionate with ourselves, secondary emotions might not arise. Secondary emotions are usually negative, since they are mediated by judgment. Secondary emotions are also unnecessary, and usually get in the way of healing because they send us into a spiral of self-blame, judgment, and shame about our emotional experience. Therefore a crucial aspect of learning emotion regulation is recognizing primary and secondary emotions, and doing our best to drop the secondary emotion by practicing acceptance and compassion.

Reducing Emotional Vulnerability

The second skill in emotion regulation is reducing emotional vulnerability. This simply means setting ourselves up for success in coping with emotions. This includes taking good care of ourselves and paying attention to The Big Three in self-care. When we are dysregulated due to inadequate sleep, poor eating habits, and not getting any exercise we are more prone to mood swings. In addition to taking care of our physical self, you can also reduce emotional vulnerability by:

- Making sure you have some down time or "me time" on a regular basis
- Avoiding toxic people in your life, or limiting your time with them

- Making a point to engage in pleasurable activities
- Planning ahead for fun things to look forward to
- Not approaching an emotionally charged subject or situation until you feel calm and centered
- Taking a "time out" if you find yourself becoming overwhelmed
- Setting limits and boundaries with friends, family, and work-related activities so you do not feel resentful and stretched

These are only examples, and anything that you do to set yourself up for emotional stability is part of this skill. Spend some time thinking about activities or habits that you feel best contribute to feelings of stability, and then work those habits into your daily routine.

Decreasing Emotional Suffering

The third skill in emotion regulation is decreasing emotional suffering. We all experience emotions that we find distressing or uncomfortable, and that is normal. There is a difference, however, from simply experiencing an emotion and being stuck in emotional suffering. Emotions lead to suffering when we cannot let go and we find ourselves dwelling in those emotions. To decrease emotional suffering, we first need to recognize it and make a choice to let it to. This doesn't mean that we can banish uncomfortable emotions through sheer force of will, but we can choose to not hold onto that emotion by delving further into it.

After we make a choice to let go, we can enable the skill of *opposite action*. Opposite action is an emotion regulation skill that means engaging in behaviors that would typify the emotion opposite to the one we are actually feeling. For example, an opposite action for feeling sad would be laughter. An opposite action for anger would be speaking in a soft voice or doing something nice for the person we are angry with. Taking opposite action creates space for new emotional experiences. Simply changing our posture and tone of voice can lessen an intense emotion.

Normalization

A very important internal tool for healing from sexual assault is normalization. Normalization is simply the process of recognizing which parts of our internal experience are normal, given our circumstances. Since trauma effects are by definition normal reactions to an abnormal event, we can remind ourselves that our thoughts and feelings are valid and expected. In the throes of trauma effects, it's easy to think we are "going crazy" or turning into a completely different person.

In these moments, reminding ourselves that our experiences are common can help us cope.

If you are working with a therapist, he or she will be an important resource for normalization. You can ask them directly about your experiences and take comfort in the fact that you are speaking to an expert that works with many different people who have experienced sexual trauma, and who knows about the common experiences of survivors.

Even if you do have a therapist, it's important to cultivate your ability to normalize for yourself. You can have a go-to phrase or sentence that you are say to yourself when you need it. Some examples are:

- I'm having a normal response to an abnormal situation
- All of these trauma effects are uncomfortable but they're normal, given what I've been through
- I'm not feeling like myself right now, but that's normal considering that I'm in a healing process
- It's normal to feel this way because all this trauma is processing through right now

Acceptance

We truly begin our healing process when we decide to have a mature and undistorted relationship with our past and present. We first need to accept that a sexual assault happened in order to begin moving beyond it. We also need to come to accept our present thoughts and feelings. Acceptance is a vital tool for healing from trauma, and for navigating our sometimes-chaotic inner world.

Acceptance is the opposite of avoidance. We try to avoid our inner thoughts and feelings if we find them uncomfortable or unacceptable. However, we find that the more we struggle against what *is*, the stronger that feeling or thought becomes. If we accept what is coming up for us, name it and have compassion for ourselves, and then move on with our day, we find that dreaded thought or feeling will fade away as something new takes its place.

Sometimes the concept of acceptance is difficult to grasp because some survivors may think that acceptance of the assault itself or its effects implies approval, justification, or minimizing of the trauma. This is not true. Acceptance is simply acknowledgment, and it does not imply that we like it, welcome it, or think it's justified. It's simply here, and there's no use saying that it's not.

Acceptance should always we paired with self-compassion and gentleness. After all, the one sitting in the midst of all that discomfort and fear is *you*, and you, most of all, deserve kindness and compassion. When practicing acceptance, you might use statements like:

- I was sexually assaulted. It happened, and I feel compassion for myself as someone who was violated and hurt very deeply.
- I notice a lot of anger coming up today. It's always uncomfortable to feel so angry, so I'll go easy on myself today knowing that I'm really angry.
- There's so much sadness in me, and I notice myself wanting to pull away from it. But I'll be gentle with myself and my sadness and simply let it be. It must be working itself through.

Your Path is Your Own

In this chapter we've explored some internal and external tools for healing. Although these tools are helpful for many survivors, everyone is an individual. You might find some of these tools work better than others or stumble across a new tool that you find helpful. You may gravitate towards the external tools more than the internal tools, or vice versa. Everyone needs to forge their own path, and I believe that everyone strives toward health and wholeness, even in our darkest times. Be open to trying something new, even if it feels clumsy or awkward at first. And when you find something helpful, practice it every day until it becomes easily accessible when you need it. And through the whole process, have compassion and be gentle with yourself.

Survivors Speak-Bethany, Age 28

I've always been a very calm person. I've never really had emotions that I felt I couldn't deal with. I've always looked at self-help books or strategies with skepticism. Honestly, this stuff looked really corny to me. All that touchy-feely stuff like meditating. I could never imagine myself doing it, or at least doing it with a straight face.

But when I was raped everything changed. It was like a new Bethany took over, and she was ready to fall apart. I was afraid when there was nothing to be afraid of. I felt anxious and depressed and had a hard time sleeping. I know now that everything I went through was very normal, but it really caught me off guard.

I remember looking online for help and thinking to myself, "This is so stupid, none of this stuff will work for me." I pictured a really cheesy woman telling me to picture a beautiful sunset or something like that. But I was really desperate. I was just beginning to think about honestly dealing with the rape, and I knew I had to hold it together enough to work at my job.

Here's what worked for me. I tackled my sleep first. I developed a routine based on information from my doctor and resources online. I went for a jog after dinner, didn't have caffeine, and read a book until I felt sleepy. I stopped beating myself up about it. I told myself it was temporary and normal. I learned how to "talk myself down" from panicking or slipping into hopelessness.

On a whim I signed up for a dance class, simply to fill time in the evenings after work. This was always the hardest time for me, because I wasn't distracted by work. I thought about setting up things with my friends, but I felt like I wanted to be alone. I ended up loving the class and it helped tire me out as well.

I read about having a mantra or inspiring phrase to use during difficult moments. I put a few up on my mirror so that I would see them every morning. At first I picked out some flowery things I found online because that seemed "therapy-like." But those really didn't resonate with who I am. Eventually I made one up. My mantra became "It sucks, and it is." That reminded me that, yes, what happened really was awful and it's okay to feel awful because of it. My mantra also reminded me that I can't change it, and I have to sit with my feelings. It wasn't very poetic, but it worked for me.

If I could tell other survivors one thing about this process it would be this: just try everything. Try it more than once. Be open to new things, because one might just work for you. It feels strange at first, but we've all done strange thing to help ourselves through bad times. It does get better. You don't have to become a different person to heal. Take what works for you and leave the rest behind.

Chapter 11: For Loved Ones

The last chapter of this book is for loved ones of survivors. The friends, parents, siblings, spouses, boyfriends and girlfriends, and co-workers who want to help and support the survivor they care about. It's difficult as a loved one to know what to say or what to do. Friends and family often see survivors at their lowest points, and they desperately want to change things for the better. It's also unfortunately true that loved ones often bear the brunt of the anger, mood swings, guilt, and shame that survivors feel. Because they are safe people in the survivor's life, they are the ones who are called upon to hold some of those difficult emotions. Whenever I talk to the loved ones of survivors, I ask them if they feel like they are walking on eggshells all the time. Heads inevitably nod. I ask if they feel like they should "fix it" but don't know how. More nodding. I ask if they feel helpless. More nods.

It's very hard to see someone we care about in such a hard place. It's all we can do to even accept that fact that our child, parent, sibling, or spouse was violated in such a cruel way. While we feel sad about the assault itself, it's also true that survivors are often difficult to deal with while they are in the process of healing. It's normal and understandable to feel overwhelmed and frustrated with a survivor's behavior. This chapter will outline some Dos and Don'ts, and explore the concept of vicarious trauma.

What's My Role?

As a loved one, your role is to be an integral part of the survivor's support system. Since sexual violence is a relational trauma, many of the survivor's struggles manifest in his or her relationships. Family and friends of survivors feel conflicted as the survivor alternately pushes them away and strives to be close to them. One man, a husband of a woman who was sexually assaulted in college, said, "It's like she's dependent one minute and wants nothing to do with me the next. It's really frustrating because I get the message that she wants me to take care of her, and then when I do she becomes angry with me and says that I'm treating her like she's wounded or broken. I can't win."

Many loved ones of survivors of sexual abuse or assault feel like they are in a losing battle. To stop engaging in the fruitless struggle, it's important to explore and define your role as a support person.

The Listener—Not the Fixer

Most loved ones ask me about the single most important thing they can do to help a survivor. My answer is always the same: you need to be a listener. It sounds very simple, but it's a difficult task to simply listen and not try to "fix" anything. When someone we love is in pain, it's natural to try to bring them out of that pain or help them identify the cause. Just like the survivor is learning to practice acceptance and to simply be with their emotions, your job is to listen and validate how they feel. When you focus on being a "fixer," the survivor is often left feeling unheard and frustrated.

When listening to your loved one, be sure to communicate that you are hearing them and validate their feelings. You can say things like:

- That must be very hard to deal with.
- I would feel the same way in your situation.
- I can see where you are coming from.
- That must be difficult, and I want you to know that I hear you and I'm here for you.

If you find yourself being pulled into "fixer mode," and you do want to make a suggestion, make sure that you ask first. You can always help your loved one to problem-solve while avoiding invalidating them. You can say, "I hear you and I wonder if you want some help with this? I could give you some suggestions but I want to make sure that would feel okay for you."

The Mirror

Our best mirrors are those people who remind us of who we are and reflect our strengths back to us when we need them. As discussed throughout this book, a particularly devastating effect of trauma is the feeling that we are not ourselves and our personality has been irrevocably changed for the worse. As a support person, you can help a survivor by reminding them of who they are underneath all the trauma and discomfort of the healing process.

Here are some ideas for being a good mirror:

- Help the survivor engage in an activity or hobby that they enjoy and are good at. For example, you could take them to the golf course or to a pottery studio.

- Remind the survivor of their strengths, and be specific. It's helpful if you can point to other difficult times in their life and remind them how they coped.

- Let the survivor know how valued they are by you. Remind them how much you appreciate your relationship with them and what makes them a good friend, family member, or spouse/partner.

The Encourager

Healing from trauma is hard work. It's exhausting and taxing. As a supporter, you can help by encouraging the survivor to continue doing their work of healing while validating how difficult the process is. Sometimes we all need a word of encouragement to continue down an uncomfortable path. Make time to encourage the survivor in your life, letting them know they can do it and that you have faith in them.

The Boundary-setter

Being involved with a survivor of sexual assault can be an all-consuming process. Keeping in mind that many trauma effects show up in relationships, it's important for you to set appropriate and healthy boundaries.

Often, a survivor feels totally overwhelmed by his or her emotions. As a natural reaction, they will lash out at a person that they feel is safe and will not abandon them. While it's an understandable process, being on the receiving end of a survivor's anger, frustration, or hopelessness can be difficult. It's important for your own self-care as a supporter to set boundaries with the survivor. It's appropriate and healthy to have time apart, or to have a "time out" if you are feeling like a punching bag or a container for all of the survivor's feelings.

If your relationship with the survivor begins to feel too strained or you are being blamed for things that are not your fault, it's important to speak up.

Here are some ideas and sentences for setting boundaries with survivors:

- I know you are upset right now, but it's not okay to speak to me that way.
- I am here for you through this process, and it's important that I get respect along the way.
- I hear you are angry, and I'm finding myself getting defensive. I need to take a little break. I am here for you and not leaving, but I am taking a time out right now.
- I'm here to listen, but I'm not the best equipped to hear all of this right now. Can you journal about this or talk to your therapist?

It can be very difficult to set boundaries with a survivor and communicate the limits around what you can hear. Setting firm boundaries while being gentle helps the survivor see what boundaries are like, and helps them learn that relationships need boundaries. Even if the survivor is hurt or angry for a time, you are modeling for them and helping them learn about boundaries.

Dos and Don'ts

As a summary and for quick reference, here are a list of Dos and Don'ts:

DO

- Be informed about sexual assault. Learn about common trauma effects and know what to expect.
- Be available, both emotionally and physically.
- Listen to your loved one if they want to talk to you.
- Help them problem-solve and offer suggestions if they are open to it, and always after listening and validating their feelings.
- Avoid any statements that may seem judgmental to the survivor; they already struggle with self-blame.
- Remind them of their strengths.
- Encourage them.
- Mirror the parts of their personality that they find positive.
- Help them engage in fun and interesting activities.
- Respect their need for boundaries and privacy.
- If the survivor is your intimate partner, make sure to talk about sexual boundaries and be patient in this area.

- Gently challenge shame and self-blame by reminding survivors that it's not their fault, and you are glad that they survived.

DON'T

- Ask too many questions about the assault itself; it's understandable to be curious or want to know, but be wary of asking questions only to help your own feelings rather than to support them.
- Treat them with kid gloves; this can re-enforce negative thinking patterns that they are 'broken' or 'damaged' in some way.
- Bring up the assault if they do not want to talk about it.
- Assume that all of their feelings are related to the assault; everyone can have a bad day.
- Try to rescue them from their feelings or "fix" them.
- Expect them to return quickly to how they were "before." Be very patient and understand that a sexual assault will change a survivor.

What about Me?

An act as devastating as a sexual assault doesn't just traumatize the survivor; it affects loved ones as well. When someone we are close to is violated, we feel violated. Just like the survivor's trust in others and the world is shattered due to an assault, their loved ones experience the same upending of their worldviews. We want to protect our loved ones, and the realization that something so horrible happened to them can leave us feeling angry and hopeless.

There's a term for the secondary trauma that loved ones experience: *vicarious trauma.* Vicarious trauma is a well-documented and valid reaction to being in close contact with trauma. It's often referred to as "the cost of caring." Signs of vicarious trauma mirror those of the survivor.

Signs and symptoms of vicarious trauma:

- Intrusive thoughts about the assault on your loved one
- Nightmares with themes of sexual assault, or watching someone you love being hurt
- Difficulty sleeping
- Disruption of regular eating patterns (either overeating or under-eating)
- Fearfulness and/or increased anxiety
- Difficulty setting boundaries between yourself and your loved one
- Feeling overly pessimistic or discouraged about the future

- Sadness and/or crying spells
- Numbing, uncomfortable feelings
- Being triggered by images of sexual assault (in movies, TV, etc.)

Just like survivors need to use self-care in their healing process, you as a support person need to take care of yourself. Self-care for loved ones includes:

- Regulating your diet, exercise, and sleep to keep yourself healthy.
- Be aware of using substances or unhealthy coping mechanisms such as overeating and alcohol. Practice moderation.
- Limit any exposure to traumatic material such as movies, TV and books.
- Separate your emotions from the survivors'. Learn to validate your own emotions, which may be different than the survivors'.
- Find outlets other than the survivor to talk about your feelings. You can look to family and friends, or support groups for loved ones.
- Use humor (when appropriate).
- Keep up with activities that you like, and make time to be with friends.

When to Get Help

Getting professional support is always an option for you as a support person. Working with a therapist or a therapy group can give you a safe space to process what is affecting you. You can also get tools and skills for coping, and learn to integrate your own vicarious trauma.

You may want to explore the option of therapy if you find you can't cope with vicarious trauma on your own. Maybe you cannot stop thinking about what happened to your loved one. Perhaps you are overwhelmed with guilt, shame, or anger. It's also common to struggle with a loss of basic trust in the world or in others. Just like a trauma survivor, it's important to seek out a specialist when looking for a therapist. You may want to have some sessions with your loved one as well, to help facilitate communication or solidify connections.

For Intimate Partners

If your spouse or intimate partner has experienced a sexual assault, there are special considerations for your relationship. Because the assault is sexual in nature, trauma can manifest within a current sexual relationship. As a partner, your challenge is to be supportive and patient while using communication and being mindful of your own needs.

If your partner is not ready for sex, take care to recognize that they are not rejecting you. They are simply too traumatized to be sexual with anyone. They may experience a fear of sex or have flashbacks of the rape when they try to be sexual. They may be so afraid of being triggered that they want to avoid being intimate. Almost every survivor I have worked with has a deep desire to be sexual with their partner, but has fears, triggers, or anxieties around sex.

You have to be patient with your partner, and let them take the lead with sexual activity. Have direct and frequent discussions about what they are comfortable with, and where they are not yet ready to go. Ask your partner how to make sex safe and comforting. Always be ready to stop if they look uncomfortable or say they want to stop. Check in with them at every step of sexual activity.

Your needs and desires are also important in this process. Make your needs known to your partner. Let them know that you are attracted to them and see them for the whole, strong person that they are. Find ways to connect even if they are not ready for sex. Be creative with how to get your needs met while you are both working through this process.

As always, therapy is an option in this area. Experienced therapists who specialize in trauma often work with couples around this issue. A professional will facilitate open and honest discussion, suggest exercises, and validate both of you.

Loved Ones Speak: Mark, Age 34

When I met my wife, I knew she was my soul mate, and I instantly loved her. We dated for two years and eventually married. We had a wonderful relationship and connection to each other. I didn't know she was a rape survivor until recently.

Her college reunion was coming up, and she became really irritable and simply wasn't acting like herself. She kept changing her mind about whether she wanted to attend the reunion. We were arguing about silly things, and she didn't want to have sex with me. I was very confused and irritated. Underneath all of that, I was really worried about her.

The reunion came and went, and she didn't end up going. About one month after that, after a long argument about who would take out the trash, she broke down crying. She said that her high school boyfriend raped her, and that the reunion had been bringing it all up for her.

I was shocked and then immediately furious. I wanted to kill this guy. I've never felt such rage. I felt like I should have protected her, even though I didn't know her at the time. I know that was an irrational thought, but I felt like I had deeply *failed as a husband. I felt so sad that she was violated.*

More than anything, I wanted to help. My wife decided to go to therapy and I supported that, going with her to her first appointment and sitting in the waiting room. She said therapy was difficult but helpful. At first I really wanted to know what she talked about in therapy, but eventually I learned to let her have that space just for her, and if she wanted to tell me anything she would.

The next few months were hard. My wife was depressed and really angry. She would get angry at the drop of a hat, and cry at a moment's notice. She literally cried over spilt milk one time when she was getting a bowl of cereal for breakfast.

I would get angry with her, which I felt really guilty about. I just wanted my wife back. We did a few sessions with her therapist together, and I learned many helpful things.

I gradually realized that I couldn't fix it for her, which is always my first instinct. I learned to avoid being her punching bag, and that healing from trauma didn't give her a free pass with all of her behaviors. The hardest thing to do was just listen to her because I wanted to help so badly. I re-framed helping as just being there.

At first it didn't occur to me that I might need to heal from this too. But my wife is like an extension of myself, and I had been violated too. I had to develop ways to stop myself from thinking about the rape. I allowed myself to feel sad and angry.

I stopped treating my wife as a 'rape victim' and just gently led her back to her life. She's always wanted to learn to rock-climb, so I signed us up for a rock gym. I made a point of telling her how strong she is, and reminding her of how she handled difficult times in the past. I began to see a lot of progress, and we re-connected. In our sex life, it was back to basics. I took small steps, and there were a lot of difficult moments.

Throughout this whole process I've seen the best and worst of my wife, although her low points were an understandable response to a horrible event. I now see that she took so much out on me because deep down she knew I would always love her.

For Loved Ones

Resources

Support Groups, Counseling and Hotlines

National Sexual Assault Hotline: 1-800-656-HOPE (4673)

Survivors of Incest Anonymous. A 12-stepp group for adult survivors of sexual abuse. www.siawso.org

Most cities and counties have a local Rape Crisis Center. You can search for one in your area at www.centers.rainn.org

Search for a therapist in your area at www.goodtherapy.org or www.therapists.psychologytoday.com. You can search for therapists that specialize in treating trauma.

Advocacy and Information

Survivors Network of those Abused by Priests (SNAP). An organization to support survivors abused by clergy. www.snapnetwork.org

The 1 in 6 Organization. Support and resources for male survivors. www.1in6.org

Victim Right Law Center, Inc. Information about legal resources for survivors. www.victimrights.org

National Sexual Violence Resource Center (NSVRC). Information, resources, and training. www.nsvrc.org

Rape, Abuse & Incest National Network (RAINN). A clearinghouse for information, advocacy and resources. www.rainn.org

Students Active for Ending Rape (SAFER). A sexual assault advocacy organization for college students. www.safercampus.org

National Association of Crime Victim Compensation Boards. A organization to help victims obtain compensation to pay for medical bills, counseling, and other expenses related to their victimization. www.nacvcb.org

Men Can Stop Rape. An organization to empower men around the issue of sexual assault. www.mencanstoprape.org

V-Day. A global organization to stop violence against women and girls. www.vday.org

Glossary

Affect without Recollection: Experiencing intense emotions related to a trauma without a memory of that trauma.

Amygdala: A brain structure found to be play a crucial role in the processing of memory and regulating emotional reactions to events.

Autonoetic Awareness: The ability to place ourselves in the past or future.

Behavioral Avoidance: Actions that are intended to help an individual avoid people, places or things that may be reminders of trauma.

Catharsis: The process of releasing strong emotions.

Cognitive: A group of psychological processes that include attention, memory, and language-base thoughts.

Cognitive Avoidance: The process of attempting to not think about a trauma; either reviewing memories or having other thoughts about trauma.

Cognitive Bias: A pattern of inferences made about other individuals or the environment created from past experience or the wish for a certain reality.

Corpus Callosum: A wide bundle of nerve fibers that connects the left and right hemispheres of the brain.

Depersonalization: The feeling of watching oneself act in the world, rather than being present in one's body and perceptions. Usually accompanied by the sense that the individual watching the action has little or no control over their behaviors.

Derealization: The perception of the external world as unreal or dreamlike.

Dissociation: Detachment from physical and emotional experience. Dissociation can be mild, such as daydreaming, or a more severe detachment that can lead to gaps in memory and attention.

Emotional Avoidance: Actively trying to avoid having emotions that relate to a trauma, such as sadness or anger.

Episodic Memory: The memory of autobiographical events that can be explicitly stated; the memories of things that happened in a particular place and time.

Explicit memory: Memory of previously learned information or previous experiences that is recalled intentionally and consciously.

Fear Extinction: The passing away of a conditioned fear after the feared stimulus is experienced multiple times with no negative consequences.

Grooming: A process by which a perpetrator draws a child victim into a relationship that the perpetrator frames a secretive and special. Eventually, the relationship becomes sexual in nature.

Hippocampus: A brain structure that plays an important role in converting present information into memories.

Hyperarousal: A heightened state of tension in the body and the mind. The hallmarks of hyperarousal are anxiety, exaggerated startle response, increased awareness to possible danger and difficulty sleeping.

Hypervigilance: An enhanced state of sensitivity to the environment, especially any sensory information that could be interpreted as threatening or dangerous.

Implicit memory: Memories related to performing a task or responding to the environment. Implicit memories guide behaviors without conscious awareness.

Medial Prefrontal Cortex: A brain region involved in the processes of learning, decision making, and complex thought.

Neurogenesis: The brain's ability to grow new neuron cells.

Neuroplasticity: A term that describe the brain's ability and tendency to change its nueral pathways due to changes in the environment, new thinking patterns, or new behaviors.

Nonpathologizing: An approach whereby a treatment provider views that patient's symptoms as adaptive within the context of the patient's life, rather than a sign of abnormality.

Numbing: An inability or decision to emotionally detach from the self and others, resulting in feeling little or no emotion.

Opposite Action: A technique for coping with difficult emotions where an individual engages in an activity that embodies the emotion opposite to the one they feel.

Primary Emotion: The first emotion that is experienced in reaction to a stressor.

Reenactment: The psychological processing of past trauma by acting out themes of the trauma in the present, usually within relationships.

Re-experiencing: The process of re-experiencing traumatic situations multiple times.

Rumination: Thinking continuously about a traumatic event in the past.

Secondary Emotion: Any emotion that is a reaction to, and dependent on, a primary emotion.

Self-efficacy: The strength or weakness of one's belief that one can reach goals and accomplish tasks.

Somatization: The tendency to both experience and express psychological distress as physical symptoms in the body.

Stress Buffering: The tendency for psychological distress to reduce in the presences of strong social support.

Temporal Binding: A process in the brain whereby stimuli is marked according to the time it occurred, allowing humans to put events in chronological order and leading to the ability to distinguish past from present.

Thalamus: A small brain structure that facilitates relaying information from the external world to the processing centers of the brain. It has also been shown to be involved with the regulation of sleep and alertness.

Unwanted Identities: Self-concepts that an individual views as negative, distasteful, or embarrassing.

Vicarious Trauma: Negative changes that occur in individual that witness or hear about trauma, or are close to a survivor of trauma.

References

Chapter 1

1. National Institute of Justice & Centers for Disease Control & Prevention. (1998). Prevalence, Incidence and Consequences of Violence against Women Survey.
2. U.S. Department of Justice. (2004). 2004 National Crime Victimization Survey.
3. Dube, S. R., et al. (2005). Long-term consequences of childhood sexual abuse by gender of victim. *American Journal of Preventive Medicine, 28,* 430-438.
4. National Sexual Violence Resource Center. *Sexual Assault Statutes in the United States.* Retrieved from http://relieffundforsexualassaultvictims.org/resources/legal.html
5. Borkenhagen, C. K. (1975, April). *American Bar Association Journal.*
6. Korte, S.M., Koolhaas, J.M., Wingfield, J.C., & McEwen, B.S. (2005). The Darwinian concept of stress: Benefits of allostasis and costs of allostatic load and the trade-offs in health and disease. *Neuroscience & Biobehavioral Reviews, 29,* 3–38.
7. Dutton, D., & Painter, S.L. (1981). Traumatic bonding: The development of emotional attachments in battered women and other relationships of intermittent abuse. *Victimology, 6,* 139-155.

Chapter 2

1. Ehlers, A., Hackmann, A. & Michael, T. (2004). Intrusive Re-experiencing in Post-Traumatic Stress Disorder: Phenomenology, Theory, and Therapy. *Memory, 12*(4), 403-415.
2. Ehlers, A., Hackmann, A., Steil, R., Clohessy, S., Wenninger, K., & Winter, H. (2002). The Nature of Intrusive Memories After Trauma: The Warning Signal Hypothesis. *Behaviour Research and Therapy, 40,* 1021-1028.
3. Ehlers, A., & Clark, D. (2000). A Cognitive Model of Post-Traumatic Stress Disorder. *Behaviour Research and Therapy, 38,* 319-345.
4. Ehlers, A., Hackmann, A., & Michael, T. (2004). Intrusive Re-experiencing in Post-Traumatic Stress Disorder: Phenomenology, Theory, and Therapy. *Memory, 12*(4), 403-415.

5. Tulving, E. (2002). Episodic Memory. *Annual Review of Psychology, 53,* 1-25.
6. Feuer, C., Nishith, P., & Resick, P. (2005). Prediction of numbing and effortful avoidance in femal rape survivors with chronic PTSD. *Journal of Traumatic Stress, 18*(2), 165-170.
7. Herman, J. (1992). *Trauma and Recovery* (pp. 52-53). New York: Basic Books, USA.
8. Tillich, P. (2000). *The Courage To Be* (2nd ed.). Yale University Press.

Chapter 3

1. American Psychiatric Association. (2013). *Diagnostic and statistical manual of mental disorders* (5th ed.). Washington, DC: Author.
2. Bradley, R., et al. (2005). A Multidimensional Meta-Analysis of Psychotherapy for PTSD. *The American Journal of Psychiatry, 162*(2).
3. Kelle, M., et al. (1992). Time to Recovery, Chronicity, and Levels of Psychopathology in Major Depression: a 5-year prospective follow-up of 431 subjects. *Archives of General Psychiatry, 49*(10), 809-816.
4. Westen, D., & Morrison, K. (2001). A Multidimensional Meta-Analysis of Treatments for Depression, Panic, and Generalized Anxiety Disorder: An Empirical Examination of the Statues of Empirically Supported Therapies. *Journal of Consulting and Clinical Psychology, 69*(6), 875-899.
5. Herman, J. (1992). Complex PTSD: A Syndrome in Survivors of Prolonged and Repeated Trauma. *Journal of Traumatic Stress, 5*(3), 377-391.
6. Ibid, p. 378.
7. Ibid, p. 379.
8. Ibid, p. 380.
9. Cunningham, J., Pearce, T., & Pearce, P. (1988). Childhood sexual abuse and medical complaints in adult women. *J Interpersonal Violence, 3,* 131– 44.
10. Herman, p. 101.
11. Kluft, R.P. (Ed.). (1985). *Childhood Antecedents of Multiple Personality Disorder.* Washington, DC: American Psychiatric Press.

12. International Society for the Study of Trauma and Dissociation. (2011). Guidelines for treating dissociative identity disorder in adults, third revision. *Journal of Trauma and Dissociation, 12*, 115-187.

13. National Alliance for Mental Illness. *Dissociative Identity Disorder*. Retrieved from http://www.nami.org/Content/ContentGroups/Helpline1/Dissociative_Identity_Disorder_%28formerly_Multiple_Personality_Disorder%29.htm

14. University of Maryland Medical Center. *Anxiety Disorders-Risk Factors*. Retrieved from http://www.umm.edu/patiented/articles/who_gets_anxiety_disorders_000028_3.htm

15. Barlow, D. H., Blanchard, E. B., Vermilyea, J. A., Vermilyea, B. B., & Di Nardo, P. A. (1986). Generalized anxiety and generalized anxiety disorder: Description and reconceptualization. *American Journal of Psychiatry, 143*, 40–44.

16. Borkovec, T. D. (1994). The nature, functions, and origins of worry. In G. Davey & F. Tallis (Eds.), *Worrying: Perspectives on Theory, Assessment, and Treatment* (pp. 5–33). New York: Wiley.

17. Eaton, W., et al. (1994). Panic and Panic Disorder in the United States. *American Journal of Psychiatry, 151*(3), 412-420.

18. Weissman, M.M., Bruce, M.L., Leaf, P.J., Florio, L.P., Holzer, C. (1991). Affective disorders. In L.N. Robins & D.A. Regier (Eds.), *Psychiatric Disorders in America: The Epidemiological Catchment Area Study* (pp 53–80). New York: Free Press.

19. Felitti, V.J. (1991). Long-term medical consequences of incest, rape and molestation. *South Med J, 84*, 328–331.

20. Walker, E.A., Katon, W.J., Hansom, J., Harrop-Griffiths, J., Holm, L., Jones, M.L., Hickok, L., Jemelka, R.P. (1992). Medical and psychiatric symptoms in women with childhood sexual abuse. *Psychosom Med, 54*, 658–664.

21. Frank, E., Turner, S. M., & Duffy, B. (1976,1979). Depressive symptoms in rape victims. *Journal of Affective Disorders,* 269-277. *Psychology, 133,* 408-413.

Chapter 4

1. Teicher, M., et al. (2004). Childhood Neglect is Associated with Reduced Corpus Callosum Area. *Biological Psychiatry, 56*, 80-85.

2. The International Society for Psychological and Social Approaches to Psychosis. *Psychological Trauma and the Brain.* Retrieved from http://www.isps-us.org/koehler/trauma_brain.html

3. Lanius, R., et al. (2001). Neural correlates of traumatic memories in posttraumatic stress disorder: A functional MRI investigation. *American Journal of Psychiatry, 158,* 1920-1922.

4. Lanius, R., Bluhm, R., Lanius, U., & Pain, C. (2005). A Review of Neuroimaging studies in PTSD: Heterogeneity of response to symptoms provocation. *Journal of Psychiatric Research, 40*(8), 709-729.

5. Shin, L., Rauch, S., & Pitman, R. (2006). Amygdala, Medial Prefrontal Cortex, and Hippocampal Function in PTSD. *Annals of the New York Academy of Sciences 1071,* 67-79.

6. Rauch,S.L., Van Der Kolk, B.A., Fisler, R.E. , et al. (1996). A symptomprovocation study of posttraumatic stress disorder using positron emission tomography and script-driven imagery. *Arch. Gen. Psychiatry, 53,* 380–387.

7. Shin, L., Rauch, S., & Pitman, R. (2006). Amygdala, Medial Prefrontal Cortex, and Hippocampal Function in PTSD. *Annals of the New York Academy of Sciences 1071,* 67-79.

8. Ibid, p. 70.

9. Gomez, F., et al. (2002). Voluntary Exercise Induces a BDNf-Mediated Mechanism that Promotes Neuroplasticity. *Journal of Neurophysiology, 88*(5), 2187-2195.

10. Brewin, C.R., Andrews, B., & Valentine, J.D. (2000). Meta-analysis of risk factors for posttraumatic stress disorder in trauma-exposed adults. *Journal of Consulting and Clinical Psychology, 68,* 748–766.

11. Cohen, S., & Wills, T.A. (1985). Stress, social support, and the buffering hypothesis. *Psychological Bulletin, 98,* 310–357.

12. Laffaye, C., Cavella, S., Drescher, K., & Rosen, C. (2008). Relationships among PTSD symptoms, social support, and support source in veterans with chronic PTSD. *Journal of Traumatic Stress, 21,* 394–401.

Chapter 5

1. Van Der Kolk, B.A., & Van Der Hart, O. (1991). The intrusive past: The flexibility of memory and the engraving of trauma. *American Imago, 48,* 425-454.

2. Van Der Kolk, B.A., et al. (1984). Nightmares and Trauma. *American Journal of Psychiatry 141,* 187-190.

---

3. Ibid, p. 188.
4. Kilpatrick, D., Veronen, L., & Best, C. (1985). Factors predicting psychological distress in rape victims. In C. Figley, *Trauma and its wake*. New York: Brunner/Mazel.
5. Loftus, E. (2005). Planting misinformation in the human mind: A 30-year investigation of the malleability of memory. *Learning and Memory, 12*, 361-366.
6. Pezdek, K., & Roe, C. (1997). The suggestibility of children's memory for being touched: planting, erasing, and changing memories. *Law. Hum. Behav. 21*, 95 – 106.
7. Briere, J., & Conte, J. (2006). Self-reported Amnesia for abuse in adults molested as children. *Journal of Traumatic Stress, 6*, 21-31.
8. Williams, L. (1995). Recovered memories of abuse in women with documented child sexual victimization histories. *Journal of Traumatic Stress, 8*, 649-673.

Chapter 6

1. Herman, J. (1997). *Trauma and Recovery* (p. 51). New York: Basic Books, USA.
2. Quas, J., Goodman, G., & Jones, D. (2003). Predictors of attributions of self-blame and internalizing behavior problems in sexually abused children. *Journal of Child Psychology and Psychiatry, 44*(5), 723-736.
3. Brown, B. *Life Lessons: Brene Brown on Shame, Courage and Vulnerability*. Retrieved from http://www.huffingtonpost.com/2013/01/24/life-lessons-shame-courage-brene-brown-_n_1967175.html

Chapter 7

1. Herman, J. (1992). *Trauma and Recovery: From Domestic Abuse to Political Terror*. New York: BasicBooks, USA.
2. Ibid.
3. Ibid, p. 112.
4. Murphy, S., et al. (1988). Rape Victims' Self-Esteem: A Longitudinal Study. *Journal of Interpersonal Violence, 13*(4), 355-370.
5. Schwartz, N., & Brand, J. (1983). Effects of Salience of Rape on Sex Role Attitudes, Trust, and Self-Esteem in Non-Raped Women. *European Journal of Social Psychology. 13*(1) 71-76.

6. Freud, S. (1921). Group psychology and analysis of the ego. (J. Strachey, Trans.) In *Complete Psychological Works, Standard Ed. Vol 18.* London: Hogarth Press, 1955.

Chapter 8

1. Herman, J. (1992). *Trauma and Recovery: From Domestic Abuse to Political Terror* (p. 155). New York: BasicBooks, USA.
2. Ibid, p. 155.
3. Ibid, p. 188.
4. Frost, Robert. (1914). "A Servant to Servants" from *North of Boston.*
5. Herman, p. 197.
6. Hayes, S., et al. (1999*). Acceptance and Commitment Therapy: An Experiential Approach to Behavior Change* (pp. 60-61). New York: The Guilford Press.
7. Rodgers, C. (1961). *On Becoming a Person* (p. 17). Boston: Houghton Mifflin Company.

Chapter 9

1. Rothbaum, B., Meadows, E., Resick, P., & Foy, D. (2000). Cognitive-Behavioral Treatment Position Paper Summary for the ISTSS Treatment Guidelines Committee. *Journal of Traumatic Stress, 13,* 558-563.
2. Foa, E., et al. (Eds). (2009). *Effective Treatments for PTSD: Second Edition* (p. 207). Guilford Press: New York.
3. Shedler, J. (2010). The Efficacy of Psychodynamic Psychotherapy. *American Psychologist.* Retrieved from http://www.apsa.org/portals/1/docs/news/JonathanShedlerStudy20 100202.pdf on July 7 2013
4. Ibid, p 100.
5. Rothbaum, B.O., Astin, M., & Marsteller, F. (2005). Prolonged Exposure Versus Eye Movement Desensitization and Reprocessing (EMDER) for Rape Victims. *Journal of Traumatic Stress, 18*(6), 607-616.
6. Foa, E., et al. (Eds). (2009). *Effective Treatments for PTSD: Second Edition* (p. 320). Guilford Press: New York.
7. Ibid, p 245.
8. Ballenger, J.C., Davidson. J.R.T., Lecrubier, Y., Nutt, D.J., Foa, E.B., Kessler, R.C., McFarlane, A.C.,& Shalev, A.Y. *(2000).*

Consensus Statement on Posttraumatic Stress Disorder from the International Consensus Group on Depression and Anxiety. *Journal of Clinical Psychiatry, 61(Suppl 5):*60-66

Chapter 10

1. Koerner, Kelly. (2012). *Doing Dialectical Behavior Therapy: A Practical Guide.* Guilford Press: New York.